# STORIES FROM THE ROAD

## ...Stories Of The Heart

the Beverly Foundation
Pasadena, California

ISBN 1-59975-249-2

**Beverly Foundation**
566 El Dorado Street, Suite 100
Pasadena, California 91101
www.beverlyfoundation.org

Editor: Helen K. Kerschner
Co-Editors: Karen Abraham, Cheryl Svensson
Format and Design: Shanna Hulme
Cover Photo: Nils-Eric Svensson

Printed in the United States at: Fidlar Doubleday

According to the U.S. Bureau of the Census, in 2003, 35 million Americans, or 12.4 percent of the total U.S. population, were aged 65 and over. The Census Bureau projects that this age group will double to 70 million people by 2030, representing 20 percent of the total population. It also projects that "oldest of the old" (those aged 85 and older) will increase from 4.2 million in 2000 to 8.9 million in 2030. In 2030 it is expected that one in five Americans will be over age 65 and one in eleven will be over age 85. According to a recent GAO report, those seniors with poor health or a disability, or who have a limited income, may face more difficulty finding and accessing transportation.

Reading the stories of volunteer drivers will tell you why they drive, but even more importantly, they will tell you why they enjoy making what many of them consider to be "the contribution of a lifetime."

# PREFACE

Quite often, transportation for an older person means more than travel to an appointment or an activity. As one person described it, "It's a journey. Travel goes to a destination; but with a journey... getting there and getting home is the fun part. There's conversation and laughter and sometimes a meal or a stop to smell the flowers."

***Stories From The Road*** is about the personal experiences of more than 245 volunteer drivers across America. The stories tell about the journey of the volunteer driver: what it's like to meet new people and new challenges; to be an advocate and a friend; to take people to life sustaining activities and life enriching activities; to drive in the local community and spend hours driving to distant appointments; to drive once or twice a month and to fill the day giving rides to people who need them; to choose to drive because of the love of driving and because it offers an opportunity to give back.

Although drivers could choose from a number of possible themes to write about, the majority emphasized "the best part of being a volunteer driver". While the drivers made valiant attempts to ensure that they stuck to their selected theme, what they really wrote about was what driving meant to them, how much they benefited from the experience, how much their passengers meant to them, and how happy they were that they had the opportunity to drive. As one driver put it...

*"When I drive, it's a good day."*

The Beverly Foundation appreciates the energy and empathy of the many drivers who wrote stories, and we regret that we weren't able to include them all. We also appreciate the efforts of the organizations that serve as the base of operations for these drivers. It is because of the hard work of organizations and staff that sponsor and operate such programs that volunteer drivers are able to not only help friends, neighbors, and complete strangers, but also to enjoy the satisfaction of making an important contribution to their community.

The stories were collected in conjunction with the Beverly Foundation's annual STAR Search survey. The name of each organization that completed a survey and each volunteer driver whose story is included in the book can be found in the appendix. We cannot begin to express the extent of our admiration for them and the work they do. We wish them much success as they continue to foster the health and well being of older adults in their communities. We also want to acknowledge the AAA Foundation for Traffic Safety and its long term partnership with the Beverly Foundation, which resulted in the early STAR Search and STAR Awards program.

*Helen Kerschner*
President and CEO
The Beverly Foundation

# Stories From The Road

# TABLE OF CONTENTS

## Appendices

# INTRODUCTION

Volunteer drivers are an increasingly critical ingredient in community based transportation services in America. As one would suspect, volunteer drivers drive... their own car, the car of a passenger, or a car that is owned by a transportation service or program. Often, however, the volunteer does more than drive a passenger from here to there.

It may be a volunteer driver who takes Mrs. Smith to the grocery store and drives Mr. Jones to the pharmacy; who helps Mr. Brown with his groceries or stays with Mrs. Taylor while she visits the doctor; who carries Mrs. Simpson's groceries into her house, or who helps Mr. Wallace into the dialysis unit; who helps Mrs. Rose to her door and helps Mr. Baylor up the steps of the van. These kinds of activities take time, sometimes require patience, and often cost money.

So, why do people volunteer to drive?

**The Volunteer Driver Experience.** The opportunity to help someone, to give back to the community, to feel needed, to do something that really matters, or to make a contribution can be a very powerful force in encouraging people to volunteer, and volunteer driving is no exception. However, it appears that volunteer drivers get a lot of satisfaction from meeting new people and sharing experiences in return for their contribution. Comments throughout the book about "the best part of being a volunteer driver" make the point.

**The Stories.** The book presents stories about the experiences of more than 245 volunteer drivers that were collected as part of a survey of volunteer driver programs across America. The volunteer drivers who completed the survey were asked to write a one or two paragraph story about one of several themes. More than 50% of the stories followed "The best part of being a volunteer driver..." theme.

**The Writers.** Who submitted the stories? The writers of the stories live in twenty-two states and come from all walks of life. They are homemakers, teachers, lawyers, doctors, students, and retirees. The majority are 55 years and over, female, college graduates, married, middle income, Caucasian, and have driven forty years or more. The primary purpose of their trips are travel for medical services. The vast majority drive on weekdays and during the day. Most drivers said they drive their own vehicle to transport passengers, spend 1-5 hours a week driving, and provide door-to-door transportation.

Many drivers say they drive to help others. A smaller number say they drive to give back to the community or to do something meaningful. A large majority report they receive the greatest satisfaction from driving, helping people, and feeling needed. Their major challenge is finding time to drive. A resounding 79% of the volunteer drivers believe they might someday become riders.

**The Book.** Every volunteer driver has a story to tell, and the drivers who contributed the stories for this book not only were generous with their experiences, they also were generous with their photographs. As you will see, some chapters are accompanied with wonderful photographs... some of drivers, some of riders, some of vehicles, and some of the members of the volunteer driver programs. The book also includes numerous testimonials about "the best part of being a volunteer driver", as well as data from survey responses. We have tried to organize the stories in groups that make sense to us... and hopefully they will make sense to you.

Individually, the stories offer a glimpse at the role of a volunteer driver. As a whole, they weave what one reader described as "a tapestry of human lives enhanced by a need presented and a service delivered." Happily, they undermine much of the "common knowledge" about volunteer driving. Many experts, for example, believe that volunteers and volunteer drivers are concerned about liability and insurance, about the expense of driving, about the burden of commitment, and about how much time it takes. However, volunteer drivers tell stories that describe their experiences as opportunities - to help and support and listen and laugh; and their contributions as helping people who, through no fault of their own, need someone to drive them so they can get where they need to go. Many of them say that they, the volunteer drivers, are the ones who really benefit.

When you read Patricia Britt's story about being a "New Wife", and Virginia Burns' story about the "Heart Attack", and Gena Morrow's story about "Cool Whip", you will have read the "winning stories." But read on, and you will discover that *Stories From The Road* will introduce you to the hearts and souls of volunteer drivers and the passengers they help. But perhaps just as compelling are the "people stories" about the passengers and why their needs for a ride enrich the lives of the people who drive them.

Photograph courtesy of
*Richard Chesbrough*

## CHAPTER 1

# BEHIND THE WHEEL
## *Who is a driver?*

*"The best part of being a volunteer driver is that the investment of a small amount of time can make a huge positive impact on the life of someone who needs transportation."*

Volunteer drivers can be just about anybody. Some are homemakers who bring their children along for the ride and others are empty nesters who are looking for something to do since after school and weekend soccer games are a thing of the past. Some are students who are just beginning their adulthood and others are retirees who have completed their paid work life. Some are people who lease big expensive luxury cars and others own old utility vans. Some are CEOs who squeeze in an hour or two a week between appointments and others are hourly employees who have more time than money. Some are mobile and run marathons and others are disabled and have to use wheel chairs and assistive devices. Some go to church every Sunday and others drive someone else to church every Sunday.

**Who Are The Volunteer Drivers?**

| | |
|---|---|
| Age 56+ | 70.0% |
| Female | 56.2% |
| College Grad | 50.0% |
| Married | 69.0% |
| 30,000+ Income | 70.0% |
| Caucasian | 95.0% |
| 50+ Yrs Driving | 52.7% |

Volunteer Driver Profile, Multiple responses allowed
*Beverly Foundation 2004 STAR Search Survey*

2

Yes, and volunteer drivers are just like you and me. They receive great satisfaction from driving someone to an important place… regardless of whether it is to a doctor's office or a hairdresser appointment. They are pleased to be appreciated whether it is a word of thanks or a jar of homemade jelly. They are happy when they spend time with a rider…whether it is an hour ride once a month or an eight hour ride three times a week. And they admit that one of the great pleasures in driving someone else is getting to know… themselves. According to one driver, "volunteer driving is a two-way street".

Another driver put it this way:

> *"The best part of being a volunteer driver is that I'm not a mere chauffeur but also a friend to my senior rider."*

## STORIES

## Dedication

An example of wholehearted dedication played out when I answered my phone one morning. It was a fellow volunteer. "Hey Virginia, can you find someone to pick up Jean in Perry? I think I am having a heart attack." "Warren" I screeched, "Have you called 911?" "Yes, they're here now. Gotta go." He hung up.

I sat by the phone, my own heart tripping double time, and ran down the list of drivers. Unable to fill in myself, I found someone who could leave immediately to collect the client for her medical appointment. I was able to reach Warren's daughter who said he was resting comfortably.

A few hours later, Warren phoned from the hospital asking if I had gotten a substitute. "Of course" I said, "That's never a problem. But how are you?" "I have to have surgery, but I'll be back soon," he said. And he was! Commitment doesn't get much better than that.

*Virginia Burns*

"***Dedication***" is a
STORY OF EXCELLENCE WINNER
*Virginia Burns, author*

## Still a Driver

Many years ago the program began in our town of about 25,000 people. Other people and I volunteered our time and the no-cost use of our vehicles to help the elderly get to the doctor, dentist, grocery store, and other destinations essential for maintaining their health and well-being.

Today I am still a volunteer driver. It is a humbling and rewarding experience. The elderly people we drivers help can no longer drive, through no fault of their own. Health problems have forced them to discontinue driving or they can no longer afford a car. The bus stop may be too far away to walk and fare is too expensive. Most are on medication. Prescription drugs are expensive and they are a must. They come from all walks of life. I've never had a passenger that I didn't like, and have made a lot of new friends. Occasionally a passenger brings home-baked goodies or sends a thank you letter after a trip. I know too that some of our passengers help others around them in their own ways as best they can.

Four years ago I began to use a wheel chair due to post-polio syndrome but driving a vehicle is no problem. Our director assigns passengers to me that do not require physical assistance. I like to think that I am still making a difference in making someone's life a bit easier by being a Car-Go volunteer driver. I feel all my trips are worthwhile.

*Edward Honcik*

## Combining Volunteering and Work

My wife is the main reason I started volunteer driving. I watched as she developed this program from the ground up and saw her dedication to getting the program started. Her dedication and desire to get this program started made me want to be a part of the program. Since I work full time, my time is very limited to drive during the week. I have been assisting the program by developing the web page for the program and helping with computer assistance. With the program just beginning, I felt a need to help with the transporting of the seniors.

My wife and family see me working as a volunteer and feel that our family is committed to see this program work. By helping and volunteering, I am showing our friends that even with my work week of 50 plus hours at work, I am able to volunteer and help others when I can. I believe this will get more volunteers to assist with drives for the seniors in our area.

*Sylvain Lacasse*

## A Change of Pace

I am sometimes asked why I continue to volunteer as a medical access driver. It took me a few years to understand the real reason.

I spent most of my adult life as professor and occasional practitioner of city planning. One of the most important lessons I learned myself and later taught my students was that almost any worthwhile project required years and sometimes decades to yield results. Some of my early volunteer work was in helping various planning efforts in my local community. This offered little satisfaction, however, since it was just an extension of what I had been doing most of my life.

Medical Access volunteering, however, offers a complete contrast to my earlier work. Here I receive an assignment, complete it the next day, and come home knowing that I have truly accomplished something useful and important to another – no waiting to see how well it comes out. Instant gratification and satisfaction!

I've met a lot of nice people both as volunteers and as clients and usually enjoy the experience of each assignment. But the real satisfaction comes from knowing at once that my time and energy was well spent helping to improve someone.

*Allan Feldt*

## It Gives Meaning to Time

Retirement, that long-awaited goal was finally here. Time for us, time to relax… time. Suddenly time was a little empty – too much time thinking only of ourselves. A note in the church paper asking for volunteer drivers was the answer.

Now, once a week, others become more important. A trip to the doctor, a grocery store visit, a pickup from the airport – all with people who have no other means of transportation.

Now, time flies by with interesting conversations about family, lifestyles, memories of days gone by and each trip always ends with profuse "thank yous" from people who really appreciate the ride. Time has so much more meaning since we became volunteer drivers.

*Bernice Knight*

## Driving to Listen

I volunteer to drive because I feel so lucky in my own life. At my age I am still able to take and give my time to help others. I frequently go to the Veteran's hospital near us and sit with patients that I take and watch other people.

The people that I transport rely on me and tell me wonderful stories of their lives. I have one particular lady that I have transported for the past several years. I feel that I know her family inside and out.

I'm just someone who can listen and put in an occasional, "Yes, I know." Without this service some elderly would not get the medical attention that is required as they have no one who can help.

*Dean Murphy*

## Helping Someone Else's Parents

The best part of being volunteer drivers is the satisfaction we get from helping our older neighbors who are no longer able to drive their own vehicles. As volunteer drivers, we meet lots of nice people and get to know a little about them and their families as we make the drives. Although it's sad to see older people gradually lose their independence, the Round Rock Caregivers volunteer driver program provides a means for these individuals to remain active in the community and live in their own homes as long as possible.

Because we moved from our home in the Midwest to Texas early in our marriage, we were not able to be there as much as we would have liked to help our parents as they aged and became more dependent on others. We feel that by being volunteer drivers, perhaps we're helping the parents of someone in a similar situation, who can't provide their parents as much care as they would like.

Who knows, perhaps we're helping someone who moved to the Midwest and left their parents in Texas.

*Tom & Phyllis Tomlinson*

*"The best part of being a volunteer driver is knowing you are helping those in the community who depend on us to go to a doctor appointment, the grocery store or to recreational activities they would otherwise be unable to attend."*

Photograph courtesy of
*Janet Bloemker*

# Chapter 2
# LIFE'S TRAVELERS
*Who are the riders?*

As seniors age, their ability to drive, to walk, or to use public transportation is often limited by reduced reaction time, deteriorating night vision, decreased ability to walk, climb, reach, or stand; or by other physical or mental limitations.

*"The best part of being a volunteer driver is the interesting people I drive. Most of my riders are kind enough to indulge my curiosity about their life story."*

Such limitations are especially common in the age 85 plus population...an age group that is expected to double (from 2,000,000 to more than 4,000,000 in the years between 2000 and 2030). It is this age group which will most probably experience a number of years of "transportation dependency" because of their inability to drive.

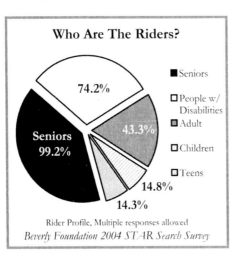

**Who Are The Riders?**

74.2%

Seniors
99.2%

43.3%

14.8%

14.3%

■ Seniors
□ People w/ Disabilities
▣ Adult
□ Children
□ Teens

Rider Profile, Multiple responses allowed
*Beverly Foundation 2004 STAR Search Survey*

In earlier times, older adults who did not drive did not need to consider volunteer driver transportation options. They could

10

look to their family members to get them where they needed to go. However changes in family structure and in the lifestyle of today's population have made it necessary for elders and their families to hope that public and para-transit agencies will be able to meet their transportation needs. Unfortunately, the very limitations that make it difficult or impossible for them to drive also make it difficult if not impossible for them to access these traditional transportation services.

While not all riders of the volunteer transportation services are in the 85+ age group, a large number are. Without the volunteer driver transportation options that are organized by churches and interfaith groups, senior centers, social and health service agencies, and area agencies on aging, these older adults would be unable to get to their life sustaining or their life enriching activities.

In this section, you will read about the seniors who, for no fault of their own, had to stop driving and had to become dependent on someone who they often didn't even know to take them places. Quite often it is not the fact that they need a ride but rather their optimism and openness and willingness to share that overcomes the problem of not being able to drive or not having family members who can help them. You also will read about some very interesting people.

According to one driver:

> *The best part of being a volunteer driver is getting to meet interesting seniors and hearing about their lives. The most unlikely appearing folks have often lived extraordinary lives and you only learn of their experiences and contributions by spending a little time with them.*

## STORIES

## Destination Diversity

As I was reflecting about the people I've driven over the years, it is amazing to see what a diverse and unique group of people they are. Much of the time I drive someone different each week. The variety in their backgrounds – places (or even country) of origin, culture, jobs or careers, family, religion, perspective on life – is always interesting to discover. How they have adjusted or adapted to the changes that have come upon them – some in a more positive way than others – has been a learning experience for me.

I am thinking now of Ella, a 90-year-old woman, whom I have driven a number of times in the past year to the same place – a "Next to New" store where she volunteers weekly. On the first drive I was amazed to hear where she was going. Still volunteering at 90! She walked slowly with a cane, but her mind was alert and she enjoyed pricing the used articles coming into the store. They loved her there and she loved going. Last week my drive to bring her to the Caregiver luncheon was cancelled because she was in the hospital with a stroke. As she continues to be in my prayers I realize even more fully the blessings and example she has been for me.

*Lois Bayer*

## Younger Than I

I picked up a woman with an oxygen tank; Sally also carried a very heavy spare, in a tote bag, "just in case" which she insisted on carrying herself. As we drove to a nearby clinic, she discussed relocating recently since her husband had passed away. She also told me she wasn't expected to live six months. However, she was in good spirits and very appreciative of her children's efforts to settle her into a comfortable apartment in North Austin. I found her remarkable.

When she came out of the clinic she was saddened by the current test results and expressed that she wished she hadn't been a smoker for years! Also she wished her farming practices had not included the use of so many chemicals. She and her husband had a large farm north of Waco. Sally was a tough woman, used to hard work, but, of course, there wasn't a thing we could do about the past.

Imagine my surprise when we exchanged birthdates and I learned that she was only a few months YOUNGER than I was.

*Susan Ledenham*

## Miles to Go...

One of my favorite riders who makes my day, is a 25 year old young man who has Leukemia. Since last December (2003) I have been driving him to Spokane for weekly medical treatments at Sacred Heart Medical Center. I drive him up on Wednesday and leave him for his treatment, returning on Thursday to pick him up and bring him back to his home (226 miles roundtrip). Starting just last month (August 2004) he now only needs treatments every other week. It is incredibly rewarding to see the efforts of his medical treatment paying off for him. He's such a pleasure to be with and he so appreciates our service.

*William Hubbard*

## A Quintet of Favorites

One won't do it! It is the fascinating mix of people that most fully enriches the volunteer experience. Hence, a *quintet* of favorite riders who "make" my typical driving day.

**Maria.** The afternoon begins with Maria, a charming Jamaica-born amputee with a warm smile, a lilting accent, and

13

an irrepressibly optimistic outlook. I convey her from the middle school where she teaches math part-time to a rehab appointment at the medical center. We discuss her students, her own current graduate study at the local university, and maybe the political issues of the day. She hobbles courageously away on her crutches, carrying her laptop computer; I feel happy and privileged.

**Ken and Kevin**. I drive to the outskirts of the adjacent community for my next pick-ups: two developmentally disabled young men homeward bound from their daily janitorial work at separate industrial plants. Ken enters first, Kevin joining us several blocks down the road. Each greets me pleasantly, and I tune in their favorite country music station. Kevin settled into his usual quietude in the back seat, while Ken commences his customary running commentary on everything from the plantings in an adjacent field to the varieties of John Deere tractors.

**Phyllis**. Now it's time for this week's adventure with Phyllis. Phyllis refuses to divulge her age beyond joking that she's not "110 yet". Our records indicate that she actually is 102. Hunched and arthritic, she walks slowly and painfully, and only with the assistance of a cane – and by clinging to the arm of her driver/escort with the determination and strength of a tiger. Once into the passenger seat, she is too short to see through any window to the outside, so she jokes: "Please tell me about anything interesting along the way, so I can appreciate it." We go to the post office, where she labors up the steps and down the hallways to make her regular mailbox check. Then we motor back to her tiny house, where I assist her to the front door and she thanks me graciously and asks me to bring more pictures next time.

**Scott**. Finally, I head into the gorgeous foothills of the Pacific Coast range to retrieve Scott from his parents' place, where he visits regularly to assist them. Scott himself is legally blind, perceiving only fields of monochromatic color. Yet, he is a computer software and programming consultant and a master of more craft-like skills than I can even imagine. He is also well-read and an engaging conversationalist, so the long ride back to town passes all too quickly.

We unload and say goodbye, and I radio my "last drop-off" mileage and start back to home base, contemplating something which might come as a surprise to many. I am tired, but contented. The contentment comes not from an awareness of what a generous contribution I'm making to the community (although passengers express both sentiments several times a day). Instead, the contentment derives from the privilege of being able to spend an entire afternoon with such diverse, lovely, fascinating people. Each one is a veritable treasure chest of talent, of charm, of richly entertaining stories, and even of mystery. And I am beneficiary of them all. What a gift: not of me to the organization and the community, but of them to me! It is just an additional guilty pleasure that everyone else seems to have it backward.

*Gary Tiedeman*

## The Real Source of Beauty

I arrived to pick up Anna for a grocery shopping trip. This was my first time to meet her. She was an older woman, but not too old. But the years had not been kind to her. Her badly dyed hair was showing at the roots; her stiff and authoritarian demeanor indicated she was once a woman in charge. We spent no less than two and a half hours in the grocery store with her endless lists. She aggravated everyone from the stock boy to the store manager to the check-out clerk. Especially the check-out clerk! She didn't know why people were always against her.

On our ride home, she confided to me that she was once a pretty woman. One envied by women and courted by men. It was a heartfelt declaration. And I heard in her tone of voice the disappointment she felt for her current state. Unwanted, unattractive, left behind. We then talked about the real source of beauty. Beauty that overrides physical appearances. Beauty that starts in the soul and comes out through a soft touch or a gentle smile or a kind word. I stayed at her apartment and helped put away two and half hours of groceries. We hugged when I left. And I wonder today if perhaps she's a bit kinder to the check-out clerk.

*Joan Tomlinson*

## An Inspiration to Everyone

There is a client in Morton, 84 years of age, who has been deaf since he was five years old. He is an inspiration to everyone.

In spite of his handicap, he supported his mom and dad and eight brothers and sisters at age 14 when his father was injured in a logging accident. He did this by entering five events in every rodeo all over the country. He has been all around cowboy champion five times.

He was Golden Glove champion once, but quit when his opponent died after a fight. He also taught himself to fly planes and do mechanic work on them. In WWII he did mechanic work on planes in the South Pacific until they knew he could fly... up in the sky he went. After the war, he broke horses and showed them. This man is good natured and never felt disadvantaged in any way.

*Mary Goforth*

## A Rider Volunteer

Frank has been very active in his long life. Recently, however, he has found it impossible to do the things he once thrived on. Volunteering at City Hall in his community gave him a unique sense of worth and satisfaction that only volunteering can do. He used to walk to City Hall to work with his comrades and helped in the office and catch up with "the gals" who worked there. They'd chat about traveling to foreign lands. Now 89, the pain in his hip from arthritis makes the mere half mile jaunt a roadblock to his cherished volunteering. That was, until I began to drive him there as part of our local "Out & About" program.

Frank now volunteers on a weekly basis and is once again reunited with "the gals" and reminisces lovingly about the travels to foreign lands. His work there makes him feel accomplished and needed. He glows when I pick him up, admitting the he got a lot done, and that the work helps to take his mind off of the pain. He thanks me over and over during our ride back home, for the valuable service I provide him. I know how important it is for him... to feel that fulfilled feeling that only volunteering can provide.

*Allison Wylot*

## The Cat's Meow

My most memorable experience as a volunteer driver happened when I took an elderly blind man to his physical therapy appointment. As I pulled into his driveway, he began walking toward my car from his porch. As I approached him, he accidentally stepped on one of his cat's tail. As the cat meowed in pain, he exclaimed, "Oh, no! which cat is that?" "The black one," I replied. Although the cat had run away by this point, he apologized, "I am so sorry, Midnight."

As I helped him to my car, I introduced myself to him. Once situated, I asked him, "Should I take the highway or is there a better route?" At that, he began telling me directions. "Turn right at the end of the street. Take a left onto..." I was truly amazed that although he could not see, he was able to navigate to his destination. In the few minutes it took to get to his appointment, he explained that he had lived in Austin his whole life and told me stories about his house. He was a very charming man, and by the time I took him home, he had thanked me many times for taking the time to help him. As I helped him out of the car, he held my hand longer, turned to me and said, "Thank you. Your help allows me to continue living in my home." His words touched my heart and brought a tear to my eye.

*Jennifer Teel*

## A Favorite Rider

A favorite rider who truly makes my day is 91 years old and still goes to play bridge two or three times a week at the Bridge Studio. When she calls for a ride, she always asks if I am available. We have become great friends and have continuous conversations to and from bridge. We talk about her family as well as mine and many other interesting subjects. She likes to make cookies and often brings some for me to enjoy.

She told me that she lost her son a few years ago, who was my age, so maybe she thinks of me as her surrogate son. The bottom line is that we, as volunteers, are helping to keep her going by giving her something to keep her active and to look forward to each day.

*Ted Riesinger*

## Socializing... It's the Bottom Line

The best part of being a volunteer driver is the satisfaction you get from helping people who need this service. You also get to know a little about them, their background, and interests. For many riders, socializing with the driver may be almost as important as the transportation.

*Jim Landkamer*

## An Uplifting Outlook

One gentleman in particular, he is a WWII veteran. He lost his left leg. When I go to pick him up, his outlook on life and our organization really is uplifting. We exchange stories, both being veterans. He tells everyone he meets about the service we provide him and his love for all our drivers and people associated with Call A Ride. People like him are genuinely appreciative of what is being done for his betterment in life. That's why I look forward to being around him.

*Gene Rust*

## A Great Rider

I have a favorite rider! She is Leah and I now enjoy her company almost daily. We met by me taking her to ARC which has enriched her life and it shows in her attitude. She is a great person who is always happy and joyful. This has made a positive influence on my life and I try to be as exuberant as her. She is trying to set a positive example for her children and that makes me happy to know she is succeeding. I hope I can continue to volunteer drive for her and many more like her.

*Melissa Elliott*

*"The best part of being a volunteer driver is being able to make new friends... People, who, for one reason or another need us to drive, suddenly are on your personal care list and you want to know how they are fairing."*

Photograph courtesy of
*William Elders*

## Chapter 3
# TWO WAY STREET
*An opportunity to give back*

Research on volunteerism says that one of the major reasons people volunteer is because they are asked. According to their stories, vol-

*"The best part of being a volunteer driver is being able to help others and to give back to the community a service that is needed and so appreciated by the riders."*

unteer drivers have a variety of reasons for volunteering. It is a way to help others whether it is a friend, a neighbor or a family member. It provides an opportunity to serve and to make a difference. It offers the means for giving time rather than money, and driving people rather than paying someone else to do it.

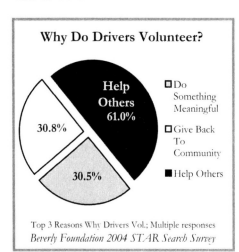

**Why Do Drivers Volunteer?**

Help Others 61.0%

30.8%

30.5%

□ Do Something Meaningful

□ Give Back To Community

■ Help Others

Top 3 Reasons Why Drivers Vol.; Multiple responses
*Beverly Foundation 2004 STAR Search Survey*

While their stories tell about rich personal experiences, heartfelt appreciation, and amazing satisfaction, what drivers really are talking about is how volunteer driving is an OPPORTUNITY…an OPPORTUNITY to meet wonderful people, an OPPORTU-NITY to have interesting experiences, an OPPORTUNITY to be lucky enough to be able to help people who need it, an OPPORTUNITY to make a contribution, an OPPORTUNITY to contribute time rather than money, an OPPORTUNITY to give back, an OPPORTUNITY to help an older person who is much like a parent who lives in a far away place, an OPPORTUNITY to meet interesting people.

Yes, driving offers many opportunities, but sometimes it simply means that…"My days are richer on the days I drive."

Another driver put it this way:

> *"The best part of being a volunteer driver is the satisfaction one receives in helping needy people. The reward derived from kindness is doubled. As Shakespeare said: 'it is twice blest, it blesseth him that gives and him that takes'. A driver's cheerful 'good morning' shows love and compassion to a lonely person, and a heartfelt 'thank you' from the rider makes the time spent worthwhile."*

## STORIES

### Thanks with a Prayer

As an RSVP Provide-A-Rider driver, I have the opportunity to meet many nice people. One woman in particular stands out in my mind. While we were driving, we chatted about our families. I mentioned that my grandson is currently serving in the army and has been in Iraq for several months. We talked about it a little, and then went on to discuss other things.

When it was time for me to drop her off after her appointment, she asked if I would mind if she said a prayer for my grandson. I told her I would be honored. Even though she can barely stand, we stood together for about three minutes while she offered prayers for my grandson, his unit, and all of our soldiers. She even asked me to provide her with the correct spelling of his name so she could ask her church group to pray for him as well. I have since driven her to several appointments and she has told me how the group at her church continues to pray for the safe return of my grandson.

And I thought I was supposed to be helping her!

*Ralph Pfenninger*

## Long Distance Talking

The best part of being a volunteer driver is the experience of meeting new and different people. Most trips are 100 miles or longer, which gives both driver and rider quite a bit of time to talk and get to know something about each other. It is interesting that there may be differing opinions on various topics; however, there is total agreement that Effingham County FISH Human Services is a gift to the communities in this county.

*Susan Elke*

## A Generous Bouquet

I was scheduled to volunteer and was particularly harried that day – my kids weren't behaving, the house was a mess, the fridge was empty, the laundry was piled high, my husband and I were in a fight. To top it off, I was getting ready to host his summer work party, and to leave the next day with his whole family on vacation. I was stressed, and I found myself muttering that I did not have time to volunteer.

The woman I picked up that day had a brief appointment a couple of miles away from her home. On the way back to her house, she began to tell me about herself. As I sat in her driveway, she admired my children. She indicated that she and her husband had married later in life and although she had desperately wanted kids, they had never been able to have them. She told me that ten years ago he had been killed instantly in a car accident by a drunk driver. She talked about how terribly she still missed him, and how lonely life had become for her sometimes. There was a beautiful tree with heart-shaped leaves in her front yard that she pointed out to me. She had planted it in front of her husband's favorite window in his memory. At the end of our visit, she proceeded into her beautiful garden and insisted on picking me a gorgeous bouquet of perennials.

That day when I returned home, my griping stopped. I hugged my kids and made up with my husband. I had a new gratitude for my life and the fights that I have been given. I feel like God spoke to me that day and gave me a gentle but much-needed attitude adjustment.

*Kimberly Birmingham*

## When I Drive, It's a Good Day

My happiest experience as a volunteer driver is one when I start the drive with a feeling of excitement… at meeting a new person, at the possibility of "clicking" with someone who has wisdom that comes only from living many years, and finding a new friend – even if for only an hour or so.

Each and every time I take a drive with a client, I meet someone who has something to say. On a good day, I find myself driving home with something to think about – it may be a sad thing about the pains and troubles that inevitably accompany the aging process. Or, on one of my truly lucky days, I will be inspired to think about life, especially a life well-lived – in good faith with the excitement and hope that each new day brings. I've found over the years, that most days when I drive, are very good days.

*Cheryl McGrath*

## Getting Out and Giving Back

I have been fortunate in my life and I wanted to give back to the community and help others. As a retired person, I was looking for something that would get me out of the house during the day. Volunteering as a driver was the answer. I began as a driver 5 years ago.

I met a woman who was wheelchair bound due to an illness. She had recently lost her husband. She was not only distraught with the loss of her husband, but also concerned without someone to help her. How was she going to cope? Her husband had done the shopping, cleaning, as well as taken her to her various doctor appointments. Her illness had left her weak with some paralysis and unable to drive. I became a volunteer driver for her.

I would take her to her doctor appointments. After a recent stay in the hospital, she developed a wound from an infection and had to go to a wound center for treatment. I was her driver. When she needed groceries for her meals, I was her driver. When she needed someone to talk, I was her driver and her friend. I was able to make her life easier. I hope I can help others with my volunteer services over the years.

*Richard Henige*

## Good for Both of Us

The best part of being a volunteer driver is helping people remain independent. I've found that most people for whom I've driven are independent types and the fact that they can't get around on their own is kind of a tough bullet to bite. By being pleasant and caring to their needs, it somehow seems to make life a bit better for them.

It, also, makes life a bit better for me, too.

*Gary Spohn*

## It's a Blessing

The best part of being a volunteer driver is the interesting people you meet. Every person I have transported has had a full life and has many interesting stories from their life experiences to tell. It is very sad to see people who were so active suddenly stricken with some illness that doesn't allow them to continue in their life style. It is difficult for them to lose their independence and have to depend on a family or friends to take them where they need or want to go.

I feel blessed by being able to make their day a little better by being able to assist them in getting to their necessary appointments, prescription shops, and stores while we are out. Sometimes we stop at a favorite fast food place for a treat they miss.

What I gain from the friendship I have with these riders far exceeds anything I could do for them. I will be available as a driver in this program as long as I am able.

*William Gillespie*

## I Have Learned So Much

The best part of being a volunteer driver is meeting the clients. So many personalities, emotions and human beings. Also the many happenings with each trip. The thoughts not only about the weather and everyday things, but opinions about everything, including doctors and medicine. I have learned many cures along with new diseases, at least to me. Many times it is necessary to literally bite my tongue or turn my head with a smile.

Each trip is an experience in itself. Overall, my twelve years are something I will always remember with fondness and pleasure. Also the many people I have met, I shall never forget. I hope I have written a little about how much being a volunteer driver has meant to me.

*Don Johnson*

## I Am the Real Beneficiary

The best part of being a volunteer driver is the personal satisfaction I derive from helping those who need help, and by doing so in a direct and immediate one-to-one way. The benefits I enjoy from the personal visits with my riders go well beyond those I get by being a blood donor or by donating money to a good cause. My riders almost always make my day better by sharing their lives with me. I learn of their experiences, their opinions, their hopes, accomplishments, joys, and disappointments. And on a rare occasion, I sense that I am able to improve my rider's day through empathetic listening and by words of appreciation and encouragement. As a result of these associations, I consider myself the beneficiary of my volunteer driving effort.

*Charles Wright*

---

*"The best part of being a volunteer driver is the good feeling I get for doing something that really matters to others. Most of the riders I have, would have no other way to get to wherever they are going. I feel that the volunteer driver program is wonderful for me as well as for our riders."*

---

Photograph courtesy of
*John Conrado*

## Chapter 4
# RIDE ALONG
*Appreciation comes in many forms*

*"The best part of being a volunteer driver is getting to know these folks. Most are shy and a bit embarrassed about what they feel is an imposition. All are grateful."*

What makes people start volunteering to drive in the first place? It may be a newspaper article or a notice in the church bulletin. It's sometimes because their service group is the sponsor or they have a friend who convinces them it is a good idea. Several drivers say they started because they had recently retired and wanted to stay involved and to do something useful. One woman said she was recently widowed and needed "people" contacts. This same reason was given by a man who said that his wife had died and that he had retired and needed something to keep him busy. However, most drivers will say that they are the real beneficiaries.

While drivers do many things other than simply driving the vehicle and providing special assistance to the riders, it appears that few are

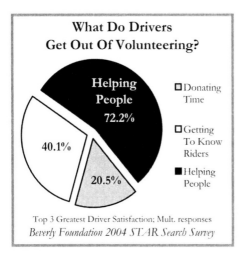

**What Do Drivers Get Out Of Volunteering?**

Helping People 72.2%

40.1%

20.5%

□ Donating Time

□ Getting To Know Riders

■ Helping People

Top 3 Greatest Driver Satisfaction; Mult. responses
*Beverly Foundation 2004 STAR Search Survey*

prepared for the outpouring of appreciation shown by the riders, and sometimes family members and others as well. One driver put it this way:

> *"The best part of being a volunteer driver is personal satisfaction one receives for providing a meaningful service that is truly appreciated."*

## STORIES

### They Depend On Us

The best part of being a volunteer driver is the sincere appreciation reflected in the positive attitude and kind words of thanks from the senior citizens when they participate in the transportation program. Every person is highly dependent upon this basic and essential service to maintain their quest critical to their quality of life: to continue to live independently in a home setting that reflects their values, respects their privacy, surrounded by the precious possessions acquired over a lifetime of irreplaceable memories.

Volunteer driving is a small contribution that can make a significant and positive difference in the life of our valued senior citizens.

*Alfred Wilke*

### People Stories

Most of my riders are kind enough to indulge my curiosity about their life story. I am often entertained during the ride with stories of life time successes, such as an opera singer who took up her profession after bearing four children; and a guitar playing engineering professor who taught himself German so he could travel and teach in Germany; and a particularly inspiring lady who played golf weekly until she was 89. Others have born amazingly successful offspring and these stories are fun too.

All of my riders are loquacious in their appreciation and that makes me beam for the rest of the day, knowing I could be of service to others.

I first volunteered for a different role, one for which there was little demand. I was doubtful that I would enjoy it when I agreed to be a driver. I love it! I keep a busy schedule, but I try to get one drive in a week. It makes me feel so good.

*Laney Hennelly*

## Good Deeds Multiply

My family and friends are very supportive and appreciative of my volunteer driving. My oldest daughter, who is 40 and has five children, has recently become a Meals-on-Wheels volunteer as a result of my volunteer activities. My other three children have also become involved in other various volunteer activities. My friends always seem supportive and comment how they think it is a wonderful thing to do for others. I am hoping I can inspire others to volunteer, as there is always a need for more to serve the community in these areas.

*Ted Riesinger*

## Life's Little Treasures

Having retired two years ago, and with my three children grown and on their own, I finally have the time to give back. I find that volunteering my time to provide transportation to those without it, makes me aware that I can actually make a difference in someone else's life.

So many elderly people are living out their lives without the benefit of family assistance. They are so grateful for the help (and the attention, just knowing that someone cares), and it is rare that I leave without their offering to pay for parking or gas, (which most of them can ill-afford) and which, of course, I refuse. But they offer, and it's like the widow's mite.

As a cancer survivor, I have received so much from so many, in terms of love and prayers and genuine concern that it has helped me become more aware of how much it means to have someone there when you need them. Most of the elderly I transport are either alone or just lonely. Giving them the exclusive focus of my attention… listening to them, giving a caring hug, and meeting a need truly makes a difference in their lives, and mine, too.

The person receiving the good deed gets a blessing, but the greatest secret of all is in knowing that the one giving is really the one receiving. I never walk away without feeling humbled.

*Emery Schriver*

## A Gift of Jelly

I have met some wonderful people driving for Volunteer Services. Sometimes I hear a lot more about family, etc., than I need to know, but I realize I am a safe person for them to unload on.

I have been reimbursed with more than one glass of homemade jelly. Clients appreciate it so much when I offer to pick up medications or stop for lunch. I like people and we meet all kinds, some not as pleasant as we might hope. But we know they are probably hurting or very lonely.

Sometimes we can be instrumental in getting more needed help for them.

*Blanche Ahrens*

## Just for the Three of Us

The most worthwhile drive was the one where I took a woman not too much older than me to her chemotherapy. I do these drives because I can't be there for my mother who lives several states away. I also have hopes that something like this will be there for me when I need it.

As I was driving this woman, I thought what a humbling experience this might be for her. She moved to Texas to live with her daughter and her daughter's employer could not let her be available to do all the drives needed. A perfect stranger came and picked her up and took her. I know she was grateful, and this felt good, but solving a big concern for her daughter also felt good. Volunteer driving is a very rewarding experience.

*Ann Bonk*

## Sharing Joy and Sadness

My happiest experiences as a volunteer driver have occurred many times. It happens when I have driven someone to a medical appointment to have a periodic recheck for some serious condition that had been under control. For example, an occurrence of cancer that is now in remission or an irregular heart beat that has been stabilized. It also happens when someone suspects something is seriously wrong with their health, has made a doctor appointment to determine just what is wrong, and comes out of the doctor's office with a smile a mile wide, and can't wait to share the good news:

"He said I'm OK for another year," or
"He said he doesn't have to see me anymore," or
"He said there is nothing to worry about."

This gives me great happiness, not only for them, but also for the privilege of being there with them so they have someone they know to share their happiness.

When the news is not good, I am still happy for the privilege of being there with them, for I can be a shoulder for them to lean on or even to cry on, a friend to sympathize with them and to encourage them to go on, a person who can provide some of the outside support we all need in times of bad news, worry and distress.

*Brian C. Irslinger*

## Time for a Talk

My favorite rider is a very elderly, frail-looking woman about five feet tall, but so very much alive. I picked her up for her morning doctor's appointment and she talked and talked during the 45 minute ride, covering topics about the weather, politics, and the economy, in that order. Since we arrived too early for the appointment because she mixed up the appointment time, we adjourned to a coffee shop and continued a conversation about our families and relationships until it was time to check back in at the doctor's office.

On the way back to her home we continued our conversation on various topics. She is such an interesting person, and she made my day.

*Richard Chesbrough*

## An Investment That Makes a Difference

Giving such a small amount of personal time makes such a big, positive impact in the lives of people who don't have an independent means of transportation.

This was brought home to me in a significant way when I was asked to take a client from our service area to Grand Rapids, with my utility trailer, to pick up a washer and dryer set. It was an hour and a half trip each way, so we had a considerable amount of time to visit.

This man is in his mid 40s and has several physical and emotional issues which have made it difficult for him to support himself much beyond a subsistence level. He shared how helpful it was to be able to talk about some of these issues while we were on the trip. He indicated that it helped to raise his level of hope and renewed his confidence that he could "make it!"

In addition to the quality time that we were able to spend together, this trip saved the client a considerable amount of money, which was very important at this time. He was facing repair bills on his old washer and dryer, plus, if he had rented a trailer and someone to haul it, that would have been an additional expense which he could not afford at that time. Partially, as a result of this experience this man is now getting additional help through counseling and employment training that is helping him in his struggle to become more self-sufficient and independent. To me, the best part of being a volunteer driver is that the investment of a small amount of time can often make a huge positive impact in the life of someone who needs transportation.

*David Draggoo*

## A Driver's Appreciation

How can I possibly relate only several special stories of my involvement in the "Out and About" program? From the beginning of my being a driver for seniors who can no longer drive, for whatever the reason, the days and hours I spend with them have been, for me, a continual time of wonderment and learning. Their youthfulness, vigor, love of life and intelligence has inspired me.

When I review my calendar each day to see if it includes a trip to the doctor, market, Costco, etc., I smile, knowing that I will be spending time with some dear people, whom I very much enjoy.

I am so blessed to have this opportunity… thank you to my driver clients for making our days brighter and fulfilled with all types of knowledge and thoughtful profound ideas.

*Owen Showalter*

*"The best part of being a volunteer driver is having the opportunity to reassess my own existence, and to truly take part in the proverbial 'win-win' situation."*

Photograph courtesy of
*Gillette K. Amidon*

## CHAPTER 5

# THE EXTRA MILE
*Drivers play many roles*

Every volunteer driver has a story to tell.  They are not stories about how much time it takes from their lives, or how much it costs them, or how difficult it is to drive, or how it interferes with other activities.  People who haven't been volunteer drivers assume those are the stories people will tell.

*"The best part of being a volunteer driver is the endless variety of challenging experiences and wonderful people encountered each and every day on the job."*

The volunteer drivers who wrote these stories say something different.  In responding to a question about their major challenges in volunteer driving, the top three challenges they selected were logistical rather than personal: (1) finding time to drive, (2) locating the destination, and (3) the traffic.

**What Are The Drivers' Major Challenges?**

| | |
|---|---|
| Time Commitment | 31.1% |
| Navigation | 16.7% |
| Traffic | 12.0% |

Top 3 Challenges Faced By Drivers
*Beverly Foundation 2004 STAR Search Survey*

It appears, however, that the rewards far outweigh the challenges.  Several drivers said they volunteered in order to help themselves or to meet people. One person said the reason he began volunteering to drive was because he was bored, another said she simply liked to drive. While one man said he wanted to build up "helper credits," another simply said he wanted to keep busy.

Often drivers said they drove because it is payback time. Many said they did it for their mom or parents who lived far away or were deceased. Some drivers said they drove because they had a license to drive, while others said that it gave them a license to do something important, to fulfill a duty, or to do the right thing.

Interestingly, while many drivers said they appreciated the opportunity to help others or to give back, most said they received as much or more than they gave.

According to one driver couple:

> *"We feel that by being volunteer drivers, perhaps we're helping the parents of someone in a similar situation, who can't provide their parents as much care as they would like."*

## STORIES

### A Great "Husband"

Ernie and I left for the V.A. Hospital at 8:00 a.m. and joined the morning commute going south. He was going to have a doctor look at a persistent wound on his toe. As the day progressed through the afternoon with a series of doctors, lab tests, X-rays, blood tests, and prescriptions, he began to fatigue. Each line was interminable. Each task was unendurable. As I wheeled him through lines, rooms, stalls, booths, and waiting rooms with the directive of "Mrs. Holcomb, take him to…", Ernie and I began to laugh at my new social status as his wife. As we worked our way into 5:00 p.m., we were taking it for granted.

Somewhere around 5:30, his patience was sorely stressed and he spoke to me sharply. A paraplegic young man came across the room in his wheel chair and firmly stated to Ernie, "Soldier, I have seen your beautiful wife care for you and push you around all day. You treat her nice, hear? You are lucky to have someone love you that much!" Ernie reacted with generosity, saying "You're right, Soldier! Thanks", and we sailed down yet another hallway in search of yet another doctor.

As we were leaving the hospital at 9:30 p.m. that night, Ernie stated that he wanted me to sit down and wait for him. He wanted to do something private. I assumed nature was calling, and I sat down to wait his return. When he came back he handed me a bag he had purchased in the gift shop. On the way to the car, I opened it to find a box of chocolate with a card which read, "to my fine wife... with thanks..." I guess you know, I cried.

The unresponsive wound became the melanoma which killed Ernie three months later. I miss him so. He was a fine "husband."

*Patricia Britt*

*"A Great 'Husband'"* is a
STORY OF EXCELLENCE WINNER
*Patricia Britt, author*

## Volunteer Drivers Are Different

I am the administrator of a program as well as a volunteer driver. We have lots of stories about the extra mile our volunteer drivers go in helping our riders. In one case where a driver was helping an elderly couple who became legally blind and could no longer drive, the driver took the husband to a doctor's office for an infected foot. When the physician wanted the patient hospitalized immediately, the driver checked him in and went back to fetch the patient's wife and stayed with the couple for two or three hours and finally drove the lady home again.

This case highlights a factor that is perhaps too often over-looked – the difference between paid and volunteer driver programs. The former could probably not have exercised the sort of individual initiative this driver displayed. Paid drivers must go by the book, or risk losing their jobs. Volunteers have more flexibility and drive because they want to.

*Carlos Luria*

## The Advocate

During seven rich years of experience volunteering at West Austin Caregivers, assisting a large diversity of older adults, I have had one experience that stands out for me in its value. The experience opened my eyes and changed my understanding of the issues associated with access to health care that face low income families.

For the particular drive, I took a physically frail and mobility-challenged woman, to a city-operated health clinic for an appointment and for medication. In a nutshell, among the issues dealt with included very lengthy waits, standing in long lines, finding out we were waiting in the wrong line, being told to see someone who had just gone on her lunch break, not finding anyone who could answer questions, knocking on random closed doors to find a specific individual to help, being turned away by the pharmacist who claimed he didn't have the medication, and witnessing the admonishing of the pharmacist by another staff member who then forced him to dispense the medication.

I feel I served as an advocate for my client as she was not able to stand in lines or search the clinic looking for someone who would answer questions. The entire experience took several hours and was unfortunately similarly repeated for many of the individuals there. I wondered how persons of limited means could afford to take significant time from low paying, perhaps hourly-wage jobs, to see a doctor. I witnessed the difficulty of negotiating complex and convoluted procedure, juggling young children during the long wait, and discerning questionable information.

This trip was worthwhile to me because now I have a story to tell, having witnessed the reality of being poor and depending on public assistance for health care. I am active with an organization that visits the State Capital during legislative sessions and advocates for children, low income families and elderly Americans. And through the years of doing this, I've learned that personal stories mean much in shaping the way a legislator votes. And now I have a specific experience to share when I ask my elected representatives to vote for streamlining enrollment in Medicaid, adequately funding health care for the poor, and doing what they can to reduce the humiliation of seeking better health. Hopefully, relating this experience will help to tip the scale toward better service for those that need the help.

*Ellen Sable*

## Something that Matters

The best part of being a volunteer driver is the good feeling I get for doing something that really matters to others. Most of the riders I have, would have no other way to get to the doctors or wherever they are going. The conversations we have may be some of the few they have had that day, as many of these people live alone. Many of the riders I have may share information they don't or can't share with others. One of my riders shared that she did all of her laundry in the kitchen sink.

I was able to follow up on that, and with assistance from the Deposit Foundation and the Binghamton Lend-A-Hand Program, she was able to get an apartment size washer. What a great feeling for me and a blessing for her!

I enjoy driving, and love talking with people, so I feel that the volunteer driver program is wonderful for me as well as for our riders.

*Mary Faigle*

## New Wheels for Joe

My senior friend, Joe, had developed a severe case of asbestos of the lungs. He could hardly breathe and required oxygen all the time now. He really needed an electric wheel chair and a lift mounted on the back of his car to haul this wheel chair. So I agreed to pay for the chair and mounting. Joe decided on the chair which best met his needs. He made the appropriate appointment to have the lift mounted on his car. So we both drove to Vista, dropped his car off as they needed it for 24 hours.

The following day, I drove Joe up to get his car. You should have seen the look on his face as we drove in and he saw the chair and lift mounted and ready to take him wherever he needed to go. The dealer demonstrated how he needed to load/unload the wheel chair and how to maneuver the lift. Joe was like a kid with a new toy! He could now go shopping with his wife, Sally and not be tied to his house.

His delight and joy was MY delight and joy in seeing him travel with his new toy!!

*John Veskerna*

## More Than a Driver

The rider was living with her relatives; two grandsons, her daughter, and her son-in-law. She told me how restricted it was, with very little privacy. She occupied one room in a mobile home with one bath. She was legally blind. She was paying rent to her daughter of approximately $400.00 each month from her social security check.

I decided to help her as much as I could. I located an apartment building with other seniors, which was subsidized by the state. I aided in filling out forms with her. In addition I used my truck to help move her belongings. Once she had settled into her apartment I never received so many thanks in my life.

Being able to help my rider gave me one of the greatest satisfactions in my life.

*John Williams, Jr.*

## Loading Up

It was my very first trip. I was to drive a man from Effingham, IL to the Danville, IL VA Hospital. All I knew about the man was his name and address, and the coordinator also gave me directions to the VA Hospital. My vehicle at the time was a minivan, with quite a high step up and the side door on the passenger side. I didn't give this a second thought because I figured the man would ride in the front seat.

Lo and behold, when he walked out of his apartment, the man was extremely rotund; actually, obese is the word. He said, "I can't get into that front seat, but the middle seat looks OK." Well, when he tried to step up, he realized that his artificial left leg was too clumsy to make it up, if he turned backward to use his right leg, he was too large to turn around to sit down. I was in a quandary! Then I noticed that the curbing at one end of the apartment complex was elevated a few inches higher than anywhere else. I told him to walk over and I'd drive; maybe it's just enough of a boost to get him in my van. He got there. I drove up as close to the curb as possible, got out and opened the sliding door. He held onto the grab bar trying to lift himself up, I put my shoulder under him in a place I'd rather not mention and (uh) (puff, pant) s-h-o-v-e-d. He was in; I was home free until the return trip. But helpers at the VA handled that.

*Joann Kroeger*

## Making a Difference

I will not use names in this story, but it is one of my most memorable rider stories. I went out in the country to pick up a lady to go to the doctor. The gate to the property was locked, and I had to get a family member to let me in. I believe this lady was in her 90's, and her family had convinced her to put her home up for sale and move in with them.

After taking her a few times, she started confiding in me. She said the kids took her car and that she was locked-in during the day. She was not allowed to eat at the table with the family, only in her room. One day I had to help her inside, and found out her room was the size of a large closet.

Things started adding up when she made the remark that her home had sold and the family was already spending the money. I finally took all this to our executive director, who notified the County protection for the elderly and in two days they had someone out there.

About a week or so later I got a call from her thanking me. She was in her own apartment at a senior assistance complex, and all of her money was in her name and put away for her needs. This has always made me feel like I made a difference.

*Billy Moberley*

## Going the Extra Mile

When I picked up Mrs. "V" to take her to the dentist, I was expecting this trip to be very similar to my other volunteer driving trips. This time, however, I gave more and received more through my volunteer efforts. On the way to the dentist's location, Mrs. "V" and I became acquainted and she told me of her many, serious health concerns. I was amazed by her optimistic outlook in spite of all her problems. While the dentist was working on her teeth, Mrs. "V's" heart rate became dangerously high and an ambulance was called. Her continued calm, optimistic demeanor was an inspiration. She assured me that I could go home and not concern myself with her situation.

I followed the ambulance to the hospital. I am so glad that I did! Her warm smile, filled with relief when she saw me in the emergency room, was worth any amount of time I may have to invest in this particular volunteer trip. Mrs. "V's" only concern appeared to be her purse. She was so thankful that I could "keep it safe" while she went through the complicated and frightening emergency room procedure. Every time I tried to express encouraging words throughout the day, she responded with warm gratitude and continued optimism and peacefulness—actually much more than what I was feeling for her! She finally was admitted to the hospital, and took great comfort in the fact that I would call her nephew, as she is a widow with no children. I went home with a thankful heart for the PRIVILEGE of having met and helped a truly inspirational little lady – better known as Mrs. "V"!

*Eldon Kaufman*

## Doing What You Can

Margaret was a lady who I had taken to appointments several times. She was handicapped, used a walker and was on oxygen – a pack she wore on her back. This one day she was quieter than usual, so I figured she didn't feel well that morning. Her appointment usually took several hours as she had treatments. When she stepped off the elevator I could tell by her face she really didn't feel well. When I got to her, she said she had orders to be admitted to the hospital.

When we got to the hospital they didn't have a room ready for her so she was told to take a chair and wait. She told me to go on home as it was late in the afternoon. She had a list of people she wanted me to call and tell them she was admitted to the hospital. I hated to leave her, but she assured me she would be all right. It was with a heavy heart that I walked away, but I prayed she would be taken care of – she was.

*Beth Holl*

## They May Not Have Anyone Else

The assignment was to take a lady into Las Vegas for a doctor appointment. When she came out of his office, she said she had to wait to see another doctor. She asked if I could feel a lump in her neck. I certainly could! The second doctor said to have her admitted to the hospital. This I did.

A week later I was assigned to pick her up from the hospital. The man with the oxygen got to her home in Boulder City before we did. After he gave his instructions to her and left, she put her arms around me and cried. "I don't know what I would have done without you", she said. She was legally blind and I was worried about her tripping over the clear oxygen tubing. So I explained how to handle it as best I could. The man hadn't said a word about it.

It's amazing to me how many people in this program have no one – no spouse, no children, no siblings, or other relatives.

*Anita Jensen*

## Random Acts of Kindness

In 1996, Evelyn retired and moved to Iowa from Maryland. She came to Iowa to live with her son. When she retired from work, she was given an option of health insurance or a life insurance retirement. Feeling she was in good health and it would not be that long until she would be entitled to Medicare, she chose the retirement life insurance. Then lo and behold a few months after she moved, she found out that she had breast cancer.

She didn't really know anyone in Iowa other than her son. She was unsure she would or could have the surgery. Getting to all of those appointments at a large university that was in another county seemed impossible to her. Through the help and support of many volunteers of which I was one, we drove her to the many chemo, radiation, and doctor appointments.

One of the volunteers who is now deceased purchased a box of "stuff" at an auction. She took out the one thing she really wanted and gave the rest of the box, which contained a lot of fabric, to Evelyn. She got her interested in making quilts. It helped to give her a positive attitude and keep her mind and hands busy through the long cold Iowa winter months.

These acts of kindness gave her the support she needed at this difficult time. I still occasionally take her for one of her checkups. She is very appreciative of her volunteers. Volunteering gives me a "good thing to do feeling!"

*Wilma Pearson*

## Appreciating Hardships

Being a volunteer driver is a challenge, as well as interesting and enlightening. You never know what a trip may bring. My most memorable experiences expanded my appreciation of the views and hardships of the elderly.

One day I overheard the doctor tell my rider that her bone cancer was terminal. On the trip home she asked my reaction to the word terminal. After taking a deep breath, my response was "We are all terminal but remember, the doctors made dire predictions ever since 1993 and you have always surprised them with your optimistic attitude and determination to survive. Just hold on to them and confound them again." Today she is much better than the doctor predicted.

My other rider refuses to believe that she has lost sight in one eye. She tells me each time I take her for a medical appointment, (at least once a week), that she is going to go into the garage, close the door, and turn on the ignition. I encourage her to tell the professionals and am assured that they feel she just needs more attention.

Fortunately there are other seniors that I transport for medical appointments that are rather routine and this gives me time to enjoy their company. These are the ones that keep me volunteering.

*Evelyn Palmer*

## Saving the Bacon

I picked up a very sweet lady for a Car-Go ride to her doctor. We got to the doctor's office in plenty of time and I was sitting with her waiting for the nurse to call her when she said, "Oh no! What time is it?" "11:20," I replied. "I forgot that I ordered Meals-on-Wheels and they will be at my house at 11:30," she said.

She suggested that I call her neighbor on my cell phone to intercept the delivery, but when I dialed there was no answer. Not wanting to cause undo concern for the Meals-on-Wheels volunteer, she became quite distraught. "What shall I do?" she lamented. "This is the first time I ever ordered Meals-on-Wheels and now I won't even be there to receive it. What will they think of me?"

So I said that I would go to her house and accept delivery. I got to her house just as the volunteer was knocking on her door. He was concerned that she was not answering and worried that something may be wrong. I took the meal and went home to put it in my refrigerator until I got the call to return to the doctor's office and take her to her house. She was very happy to have her Meals-on-Wheels dinner, nicely warmed in the microwave.

*Janet Bloemker*

*"The best part of being a volunteer driver is the opportunity to see people progress in their health status."*

Photograph courtesy of
*Janet Pease*

## CHAPTER 6

# ROAD SHOW
## *Driving can be really fun!*

What is the necessary equipment for being a volunteer driver you might ask? As we see it, volunteer drivers bring the five basic pieces of equipment with them:

*"The best part of being a volunteer driver is the people you meet. Each one has a story to tell. Seniors, especially those who live alone, enjoy talking about their family and memories of the past."*

(1) time, (2) a license, (3) logistics skills, (4) driving skills, and (5) listening skills.

Perhaps the real basics are a desire to help, a love of driving, an appreciation of people, empathy for problems, and a sense of humor. It also should be mentioned that in many volunteer driver programs, it is also important to have a car that is in good running order and to have at least the minimum insurance required by the state. With these basics, there appears to be a lot of pay-offs.

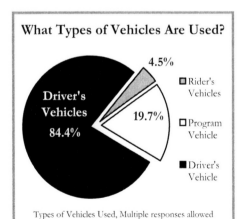

**What Types of Vehicles Are Used?**

4.5%

Driver's Vehicles 84.4%

19.7%

- Rider's Vehicles
- Program Vehicle
- Driver's Vehicle

Types of Vehicles Used, Multiple responses allowed
*Beverly Foundation 2004 STAR Search Survey*

According to one driver, the real basics are:

> *"You need at least one hour a week. You need a valid driver's license. You need to drop off or pick up an elderly passenger. You need to be a good driver. You need to be a good listener."*

## STORIES

### Cool Whip

Living in a small town, I know most, if not all, our Call A Ride clients. I find it difficult not to become emotionally involved in their personal lives. One trip, my passenger Ethel, an 80 plus year old, a past Mrs. Senior Indiana, who up until a few short years ago, still taught Sunday School, wore high-heeled shoes and makeup, always had her hair fixed, dressed very fashionably in colorful clothes, had a real zest for life, and loved to laugh. This day she seemed pretty blue and when I asked how she was doing, she shared this story with me.

Since Henry's (her husband of many years) passing, she had been very lonely and missed him terribly. She had recently received his ashes from the cremation. When I asked her what she was going to do with them, she informed me she had divided them into thirds because they had three children. I was so taken back by this, I asked, "How could you do that?" Ethel explained, "I had three Cool Whip containers. I just scooped Henry into them." By now I'm holding back a laugh and asked "Why would you do that?" Ethel's response was "Oh Henry just loved Cool Whip!" At this we both laughed.

*Gena Morrow*

---

*"**Cool Whip**"* is a
**STORY OF EXCELLENCE WINNER**
*Gena Morrow, author*

## The Heineken Maneuver

The best part of being a volunteer driver is the sense of fulfilling a need. It gives me a chance to meet a variety of people who have a variety of needs. The most important thing I have learned is that no one complains and they have accepted their problems. They look forward to their future, whatever that may be, and are so appreciative of the service we provide. If we could learn from this, it would make us a much happier and richer society.

On the light side, a lady said that she and her late husband were eating out when she choked on a piece of meat. Her husband had been in the navy and knew the "Heineken" maneuver and saved her life. And some say that beer is not good for you.

*Paul Good*

## Falling For a Laugh

Helen was a stout and heavy person. I drove her to doctor's visits. One day when arriving home, as always I stayed behind her when she went up her steps to her house. This day she got up the first step and fell backwards on top of me. We both fell to the ground, not hurt and laughing. I said, "Helen, we must stop meeting this way," and we both started laughing again.

*Ernest V. Oakley*

## I Was an "Elder-Snatcher"

I drive a mini-van one afternoon a week for Dial-A-Bus. I often carry wheelchair passengers and am designated as a "wheelchair driver." Typically riders wait for their pickup at their door, on their porch, or out in front of their houses or doctor's office. One particular afternoon Selma was my next scheduled wheelchair pick–up. I checked the address, headed out and arrived to pick up Selma at a foster home. It was a nice day and Selma was sitting in her wheelchair out on the sidewalk in front of the house. She had long white, nicely curled hair, earrings that dangled and was dressed in nondescript clothing, a little baggy. I supposed she had had a stroke by the way she sat and the look of her arms and legs.

I said my usual hello using her name and she responded with a sound, not words. It became apparent that she wasn't able to really articulate, this being typical of some of our riders. I went through the usual procedure for loading a wheelchair passenger into the van....

I opened the van side door,
put the ramp down,
backed her up the ramp and into the van,
put the wheelchair brakes on,
attached the floor hooks to each corner of the wheelchair,
put the seat belt up and around Selma and her chair,
stepped out of the van,
put the ramp back up,
closed the side door and looked up at a lady coming out of the house toward me.

She asked me if I was to pick Selma up. I told her I had Selma in the van already. She said, no that Selma was still in the house. I was totally dumbfounded and asked her if she knew who I had in the van. I opened the door and my Selma was sitting there perfectly calm. In fact, Selma was Mark. Mark lived in the foster home next door to Selma's and was just out for a stroll minding his own business when I snatched him.

I changed passengers after apologizing to Mark for the mistake and commenting on his nice hair!

*Kathy Jones*

## Lost Identity

One afternoon I was to pick up a gentleman from his home and drop him off at the senior center. He had some business in the center and was to walk across the street to the city library. Two hours after the drop off I would pick him up at the library. My client was in a bright red jacket and I had a blue jacket. Two hours in Texas and the temperature went from about 68 degrees, jacket weather, to 80 degrees, no jacket weather. We both had shed our coats in between time.

I went into the library and searched, up aisles and down aisles, looking for a red jacket, I hadn't paid any attention to his face. He was nowhere to be found. We were both looking for a jacket and not a face. Did I get scared. I'll bet no one in Caregivers had lost a client before. I went back and forth to the senior center and library, and was ready to call the police. Then I tried the library, one more time, and my plaid shirted client and I met eye to eye and we both smiled. Texas weather had played a trick on us. Was I glad to get my client back to his home.

*Mary Ann Palmer*

## The Spirit of Aging

I had driven a vanload of seniors to an art museum, and then to lunch. As we pulled out onto the highway (with plenty of leeway) from the restaurant I apparently annoyed a young driver by getting in front of him. He came up beside me, waving his fist and blowing the horn. He kept it up for quite a distance. Finally, one of my elderly passengers said "Janet, do you want each of us to hold up one finger to him?"

What a picture THAT would have made!

*Janet Pease*

## Learning Graciousness

Part of my pleasure is getting to know folks. Most are shy and a bit embarrassed about what they feel is an imposition. All are grateful. They are new friends.

One woman is totally alone in the world with no relatives, not one, and is living on a limited income with serious health problems. Her comedic version of her visit with her doctor has us laughing as we near her home. She was still smiling as she started up her walk. It was a marvelous encounter with a total stranger.

What I've learned from my riders is that I think I can accept help with graciousness if I must ask for assistance. I am grateful for the opportunity this program has afforded to express God's love and compassion for His people.

*June Phillips*

## Driving a Mattress

On a bright sunny day on June 23rd 2004 to be exact, I had one client and her twenty-two year old son. They had two appointments in Valparaiso. After leaving the last appointment, I asked if there was anything else they would like to do. She said they would like to look at a mattress. She explained she had no money to buy a mattress and there was a furniture store that had a truck out back of the store they put used mattresses on, free for the taking. I drove them behind Indiana Furniture where the big open truck was parked. The son jumped up in the truck in a single bound. He found a queen size dusty yellow mattress. He asked if we could take it with us. I told them well, today was my birthday and I couldn't think of a better way to celebrate. This was the first time the bus was used to haul furniture. I explained they had to keep it down so as not to obstruct my view.

I took it up on the lift and we all started home. We went a few blocks, the mattress popped up. I pulled over and they wrestled it back down and away we went. After a while I could hear her singing so I look back and there she was, spread eagle on the mattress on the floor. She had on a skirt with her purse on her shoulder but, she was holding it down. I wished I had a camera. It was the first time I ever saw the young man smile and he was laughing... they were certainly happy with their little treasure.

*Zenada Morrow*

*"For my riders, the socializing with the driver may be almost as important as the transportation."*

Photograph courtesy of
*Mary Faigle*

## CHAPTER 7

# THE LONG WAY HOME
*More than a destination*

The top three most frequent trips that volunteer drivers provide tend to be non emergency medical care trips, shopping trips, and personal trips such as banking, the beauty shop, and visiting friends.

*"The best part of being a volunteer driver is that you don't necessarily have to be driving the person to get the most satisfaction out of the experience. It is in the simple and most precious moments with the person that make it feel so rewarding."*

While many transportation programs emphasize what are called "life sustaining" transportation, there appears to be a trend toward providing "life enriching" or quality of life trips as well. Professionals in health and aging applaud programs that enable seniors to get "where they need to go" in the broadest sense.

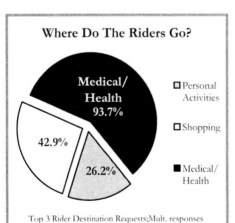

**Where Do The Riders Go?**

Medical/Health 93.7%

42.9%

26.2%

□ Personal Activities

□ Shopping

■ Medical/Health

Top 3 Rider Destination Requests;Mult. responses
*Beverly Foundation 2004 STAR Search Survey*

And how does providing transportation so that older members of the community can get to these destinations affect the drivers? The previous chart suggests some of the benefits to the drivers.

While much of the senior transportation and volunteer driver discussion emphasizes destination, it is clear that getting to a destination is not the only reason seniors need and want transportation.

According to one driver:

> *"The best part of being a volunteer driver is the experience of meeting new and different people. Most trips are 100 miles or longer, which gives both driver and rider quite a bit of time to talk and get to know something about each other."*

## STORIES

### A Special Day

One of my early trips as a volunteer driver is one that I remember as one of the happiest I ever made. The client was a very soft-spoken lady in her late eighties who resided in a Harrisonburg nursing home. A family member had called CART to see if we could transport her grandmother to a family graduation. It was at a time that the City Transit route was not operating and the family had just about given up getting her there. Since the client could not transfer her from her wheelchair, her family had resigned themselves to her not being able to attend... until they heard from CART.

When I arrived to pick up the client at the nursing home, she was radiant. Her hair had been fixed and she had on a very pretty dress. I loaded her into our accessible minivan and, as part of the small talk we made to take her mind off the tedious securing process, asked her the young graduate's name. She told me that the child graduating was her namesake! I complimented her on how pretty she looked and said that I was sure her great granddaughter would be especially pleased to have her there for such a special occasion.

At that point, she burst into tears and said that, until the day before, she had given up hope that she would get to go and that this was the happiest day in her life. I apologized for making her cry, but she assured me she was shedding tears of pure joy and would never forget how I had made it possible for her to have such a very special day! When I picked her up to go home, she asked to give me a hug and whispered to me, "Bless you; I will never forget what you have done for me today." This is a hard experience to top!

*Betty Newell*

## Counting Cheerios

I received a request to go food shopping with a senior citizen who had previously relied on neighbors as she could not afford delivery. I found she was too weak to accompany me to the store and decided to establish a consistent schedule (every other week) to do her shopping. Three trips (six weeks) later she asked to go along with me. She had gained seven pounds and felt great.

Before I started helping, she rationed her food, literally counting Cheerios and putting them in plastic bags for each day to insure she wouldn't run out. Having a reliable shopping schedule allows her to eat regularly, regain her health and eventually push the shopping cart as I scan the aisles for her favorite brands.

*John Baycich*

## The Acid Test

My happiest experience as a volunteer driver turned out to be a result of one of my most trying experiences. About a year ago, I had driven a lady to an appointment at a surgeon's office for a follow-up on an operation she had had to remove part of her colon. I was told she had terminal colon cancer and that the surgery was to prolong her life as long as possible. The trip was not very pleasant! The colostomy bag she wore was giving off odors and the poor lady was very apologetic and depressed. Of course I was depressed too, and I thought I would probably never see her again.

About eight or ten months later, I was apprehensive when the Lend A Hand Volunteer Coordinator asked if I could take the same lady into Las Vegas for another doctor visit. She was surprisingly in very good spirits when I picked her up and told me during the 30 mile drive to the surgeon's office that after her previous surgeon had refused to do anymore work on her, having considered it useless, she had found another surgeon who agreed to reattach her colon even though it was a couple of months past the usual 6 month time limit for such an operation. It was about two weeks since the operation and she was going in for a post-surgery checkup. She was feeling much better and everything now seemed to be working fine. When she came out of the doctor's office she was glowing from the report he had given her. He told her that she was a living miracle and that his tests had shown that she was healing well, was now cancer free, and could look forward to a normal life!

On the way home we stopped at a fast food restaurant to give the doctor's prognosis the acid test.

*J. Kent Longley*

## A Trucker's Compliment

The best part of being a volunteer driver is the people you meet. Each one has a story to tell. Seniors, especially those who live alone, enjoy talking about their family and their memories of the past. One lady told of homesteading in

Alaska, while another lady wrote beautiful poetry. A very nice gentleman told me of meeting his wife and courting her in his new Jaguar before going off to serve in the armed forces during World War II.

My most memorable trip was the day I was caught in a sudden snow storm. My rider was not talkative and I learned little about him. When we arrived at his home he told me he had been an over-the-road truck driver and added that I was a good driver. It's a good thing he didn't tell me his former occupation in the middle of the snow storm. People are fascinating and wonderful.

*Leona Hearne*

## Learning Humility and Patience

My happiest and saddest moments volunteering involve one client on one drive. Each week for several months I had been driving a particular woman with early-stage Alzheimer's disease. I knew I could no longer commit to driving her each week, yet I found myself in the position of avoiding telling her this.

Every Tuesday I would pick Trudy up and every Tuesday she and I would have exactly the same conversation. Upon pulling up to the stoplight close to her home, we would discuss the cloud cover and whether it might rain. About 2 miles from her home we would talk about where I lived. She wanted to know how long it took me to get to her house from my own. A little further down the road as we went up and down hills along a scenic thoroughfare in Austin, Trudy would remark about how it looked as though the houses at the tops of the hills would slide right off. And about seven times during each 30-minute drive, she would say, "This is a LONG way for you to go all the way up here and all the way back."

The conversation continued pleasantly, if repetitiously. She adored my 2-year-old son, each week meeting him for the first time. I could not tell her that I would not be seeing her each week anymore. I felt the message would unnecessarily upset her for a moment then promptly disappear from her mind, so why bother?

This weekly drive taught me humility and patience. I also learned from Trudy, one of the most pleasant people I have met, that a positive attitude eclipses human weakness.

*Sarah Carriker*

## Providing Human Contact

You meet so many people who have lived interesting and even exciting lives, and they delight in having an audience to whom they can tell their stories. One elderly woman that I drove had been a resident here from birth, and made me wish she had lived further away, so I could hear more. She regaled me with vignettes of Austin in earlier years, including the delight of going to Barton Springs in a surrey with the fringe on top.

Early on in my volunteer driving, I realized that listening to and interacting with our clients, many of whom have little out-side human contact, is almost as important to their well being as driving them to their destination.

*John Conrado*

## The Beauty Shop

I have been given the opportunity to spend quality time with a very special lady. I drive her to the same beauty shop she has gone to for over 30 years!

The weekly trips provide both of us the chance for personal discussion about our families and most important, church family.

I'm proud to be a part of the WAC organization that provides this volunteer driver program for our senior community.

*Olivia Donelson*

*"The best part of being a volunteer driver is when one of your passengers asks if you will go to lunch with them. A lot of our passengers live alone and/or are sick. They enjoy talking to someone and sharing a meal."*

Photograph courtesy of
*J. Kent Longley*

## CHAPTER 8

# PASSAGES

*Experiencing the alternative*

"*A valuable lesson to be learned from this experience is that one person can make a difference in the lives of people who are coping with health problems, disabilities and loneliness if we just reach out to them with compassion. It can be a very rewarding experience.*"

Volunteer drivers understand when they enter a driving program that their riders are often frail, in poor health, and may not have a long time to live. This does not stop them from volunteering their time and efforts to help riders access the medical treatments they need in order to live pain free as long as possible. In this sense, they are courageous because by facing the possibility of the death of another, they are facing their own fear of death and this strengthens them to live their own life fully.

## What Type of Assistance Do Riders Need?

| | |
|---|---|
| Hand-to-Hand | 86.3% |
| Escort Service | 77.6% |
| Door-to-Door | 90.4% |
| Door-thru-Door | 62.6% |

Assistance To Riders, Multiple responses allowed
*Beverly Foundation 2004 STAR Search Survey*

The stories in this chapter express the great rewards and joy that are often the result of driving a frail older client and getting to know them as a person. Humor and sto-

ries of one's life, shared interests, hopes and fears are the ties
that bind driver and rider during their trips together. There is
a saying that getting old is better than the alternative... But in
the vernacular of transportation, "at some point, people simply run out of steam". While they don't talk about it a lot,
many drivers say they experience the sadness of losing a dear
friend when a passenger dies. Even though they may lose a
friend, they all report the privilege it was to know the rider
and the many benefits they reaped from the friendship. However, the story generally doesn't end there, for the driver often
continues to provide rides to others who need them.

It appears that volunteer drivers look at the special assistance
they provide as a rewarding experience rather than a burden.

According to one driver:

> *"The best part of being a volunteer driver is meeting a lot of
> good people, some are very sick. At those times I thank God
> for my good health."*

## STORIES

### A Tear for a Friend

The first time I met Mr. Markwick was a comforting one to
me because he was just an ordinary guy. We hit it off really
well because we had a similar interest, NASCAR racing, and
we both liked Ford drivers. It was a pleasant drive from his
home to dialysis and back and I especially enjoyed getting him
a wheelchair and pushing him to the room where his blood
was going to be cleansed by machine. The reason why he
needed a "joyride" in a wheelchair was due to his emphysema.
When we rode home in the afternoon, we enjoyed listening to

Dave Ramsey and his financial advice on the radio. It sure was an interesting year transporting Mr. Markwick.

One Saturday, I went to pick him up and found out that he wasn't feeling too well. I didn't think much of it, but felt a little sadness for him. Later on, I learned that he suffered a heart attack and was in the hospital. A few days later, he passed away. I felt bad that I had lost a valuable friend that had made my job as a volunteer driver a very enjoyable one. Drops of moisture may have welled up in my eyes, cleaning them and giving me a new vision for driving other clients in the future.

*Tom King*

## Proud to the End

Because the people we drive are either elderly or sick or both, we know that it is inevitable that we are going to lose some of them over the course of time. In my seven-year tenure with the Volunteer Center of Jefferson County, New York, I have lost over a dozen clients to various causes. I became friends with most of them because due to the chronic nature of their illnesses, I drove them frequently, in many cases traveling as far as one hundred nine miles round trip. When you spend three hours together in the confines of a car, and do it on a regular basis, you often become close whether you intend to or not.

I can tell many such stories, but the saddest one involves a woman named Mary whom I first met when the Volunteer center asked me to take her to a clinic eighty-five miles away. It was a snowy winter day, and when I arrived at her house, I noticed that her walk had not been shoveled. Naturally, I offered to shovel for her, but she refused exclaiming, "I'm only eight-four years old. I'm perfectly capable of shoveling my own walks. I'll do it when I get home." I liked her immediately. She was fiercely independent, stubbornly proud, and had a sharp wit coupled with a warm sense of humor. Over the course of our many trips together, we discussed religion, politics, books we had read, finances, our late spouses, our families, love, life, and death. It was during one of our trips that I learned that her twenty-three-year-old granddaughter was terminally ill with cancer. She died a short time later. I remember Mary saying how unfair life was and how she wished it had been she rather than her granddaughter. Within a year Mary got her wish. Her kidneys were failing and dialysis was the only option. In typical fashion Mary refused saying, "I'm eighty-seven years old. I've lived long enough."

I saw Mary two days before she died. She told me that there would be no wake and no funeral. I said, "Mary, don't you want people to get up at your funeral and say nice things about you?" She replied, "If people couldn't say nice things about me when I was alive, I don't want them saying them when I'm dead." She smiled and told me not to cry over her and to get on with my life. I left with tears streaming down my cheeks.

*Charles Lehman*

## The Ladies Next Door

Since the Pflugerville Caregivers has only been in operation for two weeks, I have driven only twice for this organization. However, I have driven on my own to assist several senior citizens in this capacity.

Most noteworthy were my next door neighbors, two elderly ladies named Davie and Dillie who were twins. After Davie was confined to a nursing home about forty miles away, I would pick up Dillie from next door and drive her to visit her sister. After the visit, which sometimes had its ups and downs, we drove along a pleasant country road stopping for lunch at a

Dairy Queen. Then we proceeded to another town to visit with the twins' three older siblings who were still living together in their own home. We took this trip a few times before Davie passed away. About a year later Dillie died as well. But I will always fondly remember the "ladies next door" and feel blessed to have been of service to them.

*Sharion Tanner*

## It Was a Privilege

Thelma, a widow I transported to and from dialysis, was my favorite rider who always made my day. Thelma had an upbeat attitude and very positive outlook on life. She knew the severity of her situation and had made definite plans for when her condition worsened. She lost her husband just the year before I met her. Thelma realized that she had to be on dialysis or die, but nothing could change her spicy attitude.

Each time I took her for her treatment she had a funny story or joke to tell me. Needless to say, our trips were full of laughter and I always looked forward to them. We had a couple of serious talks and she shared what her plan was for the time her doctor talked "surgery." Not one to mince words, she planned to tell him: "No way! I've had a good life, had a great time and I'm ready to be free of the pain." And so it was. She is gone now and I miss her lighthearted banter. Thelma was a joy to know and I appreciate the privilege.

*Winifred Healey*

## A Sad Trip

As a volunteer driver, I enjoy the one-on-one contact I have with the clients I drive to appointments. Each one has his/her own personality and most are very enjoyable to be around. The saddest experience I had as a volunteer driver was taking a client to the hospital. Within two weeks of that trip, he passed away of cancer.

I never have taken a client I didn't like. Some are more challenging but I get along with all of them.

*Margaret Johnston*

## She Touched My Heart

About five years ago I started picking up a woman at the University Hospital in Iowa City one day a week and returning her to her home in Tipton for the Volunteer Services of Cedar County under the capable direction of Elda Licht. This rider was what I would call "gruff". She used some of the most vulgar language I had ever heard and complained almost incessantly. Later she had to be transported from her apartment to the car and into the hospital in a wheel chair in all kinds of weather including icy weather when sidewalks had not been cleared.

After an experience of her vomiting in my car, I learned to always carry a pan in the car. To say the least she was a challenge. In order to divert her attention from herself and her many ailments, I tried to take different routes from her home to the hospital and later from the hospital to her home when she was no longer able to ride the SEAT bus.

During an appropriate season, I would point out beautiful blooming flowers, trees in a riot of fall color, or a herd of cattle with new baby calves or a deer along the way. After two or three years of this, I noticed she began calling my attention to things of beauty or interest and her language became less vulgar and complaining despite increasing suffering. The last summer she was alive, a friend had given her more beets than she could use herself, so she offered me a jar of beets she had canned, showing a more giving spirit. At Christmas time I was one of five to receive a card. That was her way of saying a big thank you with her meager means to "one of her favorite drivers" for the years of transporting her to and from her medical appointments that no doubt extended her life a few more years.

My thanks to Elda Licht, coordinator for the Volunteer Services for Cedar County, for giving me this opportunity to make a difference in the life of one rider.

*Clara Millett*

## My Saddest Experience as a Volunteer Driver

Several years ago I took a Reserve Colonel Air Force Nurse to appointments. She had participated in air evacuations from Viet Nam and also Afghanistan and had contracted cancer from being exposed to Agent Orange.

I witnessed her growing weaker and having more treatments. She had a very positive outlook and had prepared a documentary film on Flight Nurses and was planning another one.

Even when she eventually went into hospice care she said that it was only until she became strong enough to go home. I still miss her.

*Catharine F. Edgerton*

## In Memory of Mom

The best part of being a volunteer driver is being able to help the homebound elderly get to their medical appointments. Most do not have family close by or available to provide transportation to appointments. Regular visits to a doctor are necessary for them to maintain good health and to allow them to continue to live independently. They are very grateful for the rides I provide. We become good friends and look forward to our trips together, because we share our thoughts on a myriad of subjects. Most of my riders love to talk about the Red Sox!

I took care of my mother for several years before she passed away. After that I decided that in memory of my mother I would volunteer to drive for seniors. I know my mom would be very happy to know that because of her I am helping other seniors.

*Barbara Stokoe*

## Unforeseen Consequences

My most memorable experience as a volunteer driver for the Retired and Senior Volunteer Program of Schuylkill County, Pennsylvania, occurred, strange as it may seem, at the wake for a lady whom I had driven to a long, but unfortunately unsuccessful, series of chemotherapy treatments.

I had met the lady when I drove her to an earlier medical testing session and knew that she was a widow with no children and whose nearest relatives all lived a distance away in other states. These tests showed the need for a series of chemotherapy treatments. I knew how rough these treatments can sometimes be for a person, particularly for a person living alone without others to support them physically and emotionally, so I agreed to drive her to and from the appointments, stay with her during the treatments, and make sure that she was in good enough shape to be left home alone when we returned from the treatments. I took her to about a dozen treatments over the next six months, and called her occasionally between treatments and after the treatments were finished to see how she was doing. I also dropped by to pay her a short visit a couple of times when I was in her neighborhood. We enjoyed each other's company; she seemed to like my light hearted, joking approach to life; and I had nothing but respect for this brave lady who never once complained about any of the many things she had every right to constantly complain about. As time went on it became obvious that she was getting worse; and finally I received a call from her niece, who had come from Ohio to be with her at the end, informing me that she had passed away.

When I went to her wake, I was very surprised to have many of her relatives, neighbors and friends come over to meet me and to tell me how often she had talked about me and about how comforting and helpful to her our various contacts had been. Her brother invited me to serve as a pallbearer at her funeral, which I was honored to do. Here I was berating myself internally for not having found time to call and visit her more often, while she had been praising me to everyone for the little that I had done for her. What a joy it is to know that you have been able to make a difference in someone else's life; or that something you did for someone else worked out even better than you thought it would.

Incidentally, some might consider this a sad story because it ended in death; I do not. In working with the elderly we must realize that some of them will be leaving us soon while others will probably be around for a good long while yet. I maintain that giving aid and comfort to those who will soon be leaving this life is just as important as helping those we expect to still be around for a while.

*Brian C. Irslinger*

## A Strange Coincidence

I met George on the golf course. Although we never played together and never knew each other's name, we always talked and joked about our game. I received a call one day to pick up a person and take him to dialysis. When I arrived at his house, it was George. I drove him twice a week for a year and half to and from dialysis and we became good friends. I met some of his family and we talked about playing golf together.

One day I received a call from his wife telling me not to pick up George anymore for he had passed away. I still think of him and the talks we had together.

*Ernest V. Oakley*

## A Christmas Gift

In 1996, I met Cindy and her two children at church. At the time, Cindy had MS, but was still fairly independent. Over the course of time, we became friends. In 1998, the disease affected her mobility to the point that she was placed in a nursing home in a neighboring county some 70 miles away, and her children were sent to Omaha to live with her brother. Another friend and I struggled to find and arrange transportation for Cindy. Someone suggested that we contact a local taxi company. When I approached the owner of the taxi company, he "recruited" me to be a volunteer driver for CART.

Christmas of 2000 soon approached. Cindy had not been home or seen her children in two years. Transportation was a major barrier unless she traveled by emergency services at a great cost. Through CART, I was able to bring Cindy home for Christmas and see her children for the first time in two years. By far, that was the most memorable trip I ever made as a volunteer driver. Although Cindy is no longer with us, this trip brought another blessing – Cindy's mother signed up as a volunteer driver.

*Dariek Calloway*

"*As one person described it, 'It's a journey.' Travel gets you from here to there. But a journey…getting there and getting home is the fun part. There's conversation and laughter and sometimes a meal or a stop to smell the flowers.*"

Photograph courtesy of
*Gary Tiedeman*

## CHAPTER 9

# THE HIGH ROAD

*I am inspired*

*"The best part of being a volunteer driver is the people I have met, all of whom have enriched my life. I have been stretched, changed, educated, challenged, and humbled in many ways..."*

There is a saying that "volunteer drivers are the hardest volunteers to recruit, but once you've got them, you've got them". One of the reasons is that volunteer drivers often say they receive more from their experience than they give.

But what is it about recruiting drivers that is so difficult? Drivers express concerns about liability and insurance, time requirements, medical emergencies, cost of gasoline, and so on. Sponsoring organizations say that in many cases simply asking a person is enough to overcome many fears and that most other concerns are overcome during driver orientation. There appears to be general agreement

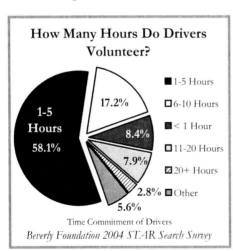

**How Many Hours Do Drivers Volunteer?**

- ■ 1-5 Hours
- □ 6-10 Hours
- ■ < 1 Hour
- □ 11-20 Hours
- ▨ 20+ Hours
- ■ Other

1-5 Hours 58.1%

17.2%

8.4%

7.9%

2.8%

5.6%

Time Commitment of Drivers
*Beverly Foundation 2004 STAR Search Survey*

that if fears about volunteer driving persist they may actually be an excuse for not driving.

However, once they get started, they tend to be volunteer drivers for a long period of time. The reasons are simple: it is a time for helping people, for meeting new and interesting people, to give back, to serve, to enable seniors to stay in their homes, to give time rather than money, to do something meaningful, to stay involved.

Perhaps Karen MacMurtrie said it best.

> *"The best part of being a volunteer driver is having an opportunity to meet new and interesting people... who so desperately want to maintain their independence. These are people who have had rich lives and enjoy sharing a bit of their experience in exchange for a lift. They may not know it but they inspire me in ways that can't be defined."*

## STORIES

### A Gift of History

As a volunteer driver for West Austin Caregivers, I like to feel like I am giving something to the clients I drive. One day, however, I felt as if I were given a wonderful gift from a client.

I drove to a nice, older section of town to pick up my client and take her grocery shopping. When she answered the door, she was not quite ready to go. She invited me to come in and chat with her husband for a minute. After she had introduced us, she suggested that he show me some photos. As we walked down the hallway, there were hundreds of photos. Many were family pictures. Others were of the husband serving in the Navy. But the ones that most captured my attention were pictures of the two of them at the White House and the Capitol Building. The husband had served as a U.S. Congressman from New York. There were pictures of him with former presidents, including Dwight Eisenhower. There were pictures of him with famous actors and actresses and even one with Golda Meir. This man had served his country in the U.S. Navy, and then gone on to serve in Congress. It was an amazing walk through history, and I loved his personal stories that he shared as I asked about the photos.

As his wife came back and was ready to go, I was sad that my history lesson was over. She lovingly patted him and reminded him to drink his juice. He kissed her sweetly good-bye and we left.

Later, we returned home and I helped carry their groceries into the kitchen. They both thanked me profusely for the ride to the store. I thanked them for a wonderful visit and silently hoped I might drive them again.

*Carla Robertson*

## Through Good Times and Bad

I suppose my favorite rider would be the choice of several of the Call A Ride drivers. June is a gem. She suffers from kidney disease and must endure dialysis three times a week, which makes her the most "regular" client we serve.

Through good times and bad, June remains cheerfully optimistic. She never fails to thank and praise the volunteer drivers who literally keep her alive. Her years of treatment remind me on a monthly basis to be thankful for the health I enjoy that makes it possible for me to serve her and our other clients.

*Margaret Lukas*

## I Am Honored

When I arrived at his home both he and his wife were dressed in "proper" business attire and were awaiting my arrival. The client was a distinguished looking gentleman in his mid 80's. He showed the signs of having worked hard his entire life, he was crippled with arthritis, experiencing some difficulty breathing, blind, and in the process of fighting cancer.

Very few words were spoken other than the general niceties until he was seated and we started off. Suddenly the gentleman stated "I was in World War II". His wife made a facial expression to indicate that she had heard this all before. I said to him "I'll bet you have some stories". At which point he started speaking and reliving some of his past experiences.

I dropped him off at his doctor's and anxiously awaited the trip home. I took the longest route back to his house and even stopped to allow his wife an opportunity to shop for some groceries. He talked almost continuously but never spoke ill of anyone or of the burdens he was carrying. I realized then that I was honored to be in the presence of a truly great man.

*Kenneth Fuerst*

## A Special Privilege

It is difficult to single out one event or instance in my fourteen years of volunteer driving. I do know this: I make a difference in the lives of those with whom I come in contact as a volunteer driver. I often feel that I am a part of their family. They look forward to seeing me when I pick them up. They are anxious to share their family experiences with me. We get to know what is important in our family lives. In some cases, I may be the only person they speak to in a period of time.

They and I look forward to these discussions. I wouldn't go quite as far as saying that my being a volunteer driver has changed my life nor my rider's life, but it certainly adds another dimension to our lives. I most certainly look forward to those days when I drive whether it is to take them to doctor's appointments or to special events in their lives.

It is a special privilege. Being a volunteer driver has been everything that I hoped it would be.

*William Bones*

## Beautiful Memories

Although each rider has a unique personality, one in particular stands out as a favorite. Helen was forgetful, but she was always glad to see me on Monday afternoons at 4:00 when I would pick her up from an adult day-care program to drive her home. When we walked out the door to get into my plain gray minivan, she would often exclaim over my vehicle: "Oh, I get to ride in this! How nice!" Her gracious demeanor and gratitude for the ride home was consistent, and I looked forward to our time together.

During the ride home, Helen would notice the beauty of the flowers, changing leaves, or farmers' fields, depending upon the season. Although she lamented her loss of memory, most of our conversation revolved around anything and everything, from childhood memories to the outrageous price of gasoline to her sister's wonderful cooking. She repeated herself often, but I answered each question patiently. I never tired of hearing the pride in her voice when she told me that her brother made the winning basket when his high school team won the state championship in 1940. After taking Helen to her home, I would feel that I was truly blessed. She always made my day.

*Margaret Gehling*

## Setting an Example

As a working woman in the early 1990's, I had the pleasure of serving a variety of people in the Knoxville area through Project LIVE. The Volunteer Coordinator then was a wonderful lady named "Mary Ann." She eventually set me up with "Ann," a funny spinster who began calling me directly when she needed groceries, banking or medicines. After a few years, Ann moved into a nursing home and my job situation changed, so I quit volunteering for a time. Our two daughters, named after their great grandmothers, were part of the reason I began volunteering again. I believe that I cannot expect our children to have a heart for service, or a heart for our senior citizens, unless we teach them to. And the only way to teach them is by example.

Fast forward to 2002 and I began volunteering again—this time with our girls in the backseat. And the most delightful thing has happened—not only do I get the privilege of driving "Mary Ann" (that same volunteer coordinator who helped so many people long ago)—I get to see her smile when my daughters give her a hug good-bye.

The best part about being a volunteer driver? Giving Mary Ann and others like her the chance to stay independent for as long as they're able. And giving my children the chance to develop a heart for service.

*Bonnie Marret*

## Inner Beauty

I drove an elderly man, probably in his eighties, to a hospital in a nearby city for radiation treatment for cancer.

We talked about the things that often come up in conversations between older people, the things that have mattered most in lives well lived. The stories he told me about his own life have stayed with me, memorable and inspiring.

He had spent his early life in poverty with his family on a houseboat, surviving the depression with good spirit and little regret. As a young man he had studied interior decoration and had become a very successful designer, working for many years as the chief interior designer for a large developer.

He invited me into his home. It was appealing and reflected his own good taste and artistic sophistication of his profession. The home had once been an old store that he had completely remodeled and decorated. Once again he succeeded in bringing something barren and unadorned, like his own childhood, into an experience of serene beauty, much like the spirit of this man.

*Gordon Easlick*

## Learning from My Elders

In the car we gossip about people we know. I find out news about Hong Kong from my riders. It's an enjoyable learning experience about life in general.

I also get medical knowledge and learn about superstition and Chinese cultural traditions. It's an eye opener for me as an American Chinese who has been brought up in the U.S. I learn about Chinese culture from my elderly riders.

*Lila Jue*

## The People I Meet

In the past four years I have had a variety of riders and a few recognizable names as I start to get assigned some repeat customers. What I like best about driving is meeting the variety of people who so desperately want to maintain their independence. These are people who have had rich lives and enjoy sharing a bit of their experience in exchange for a lift.

I have met retired teachers, a Rabbi, a musician, widows and grandparents. They are from a variety of ethnic backgrounds and diverse geographies. Their bodies may not work as smoothly as they may have, but their minds are full of memories, insights and experiences. They are typically so appreciative when I feel I have done so little.

They may not know it but they inspire me in ways that can't be defined. My days are richer on the days I drive. And for this I have them to thank.

*Karen MacMurtrie*

## I Hope I Can Be Like Them

The individuals I drive are a real inspiration to me. Probably 80% of my drives are to doctor appointments, and with few exceptions my riders are upbeat and optimistic about the future. Many in their upper 80's are involved in all sorts of activities; life is still meaningful, and they feel they have an important contribution to make.

I just hope as I rapidly move into this arena, I will be like my new friends I have met through driving several times a week, and sometimes a bit more!  It really makes a guy like me want to give them my best, which then flows directly to the clients. I just hope they will still be around when I no longer can be a driver and become a client!!

*John Scurlock*

## I Am Humbled

Helping Interfaith Volunteer Caregiver clients maintain their independence is the best part of being a driver. When I took my driver's road test many years ago, I thought I would drive forever. Most of the clients probably had the same thought. Then one day a family member, doctor, or perhaps a minister, said, "You can no longer drive." Independence is gone. Now what? That is where we come in.

My riders thank me over and over for driving them to their destinations. I am humbled. Being a volunteer driver is one of the greatest gifts I can give to members of my community. I have never met a rider I wouldn't want to bring home and share with my family.

In other words – my riders and their continued independence is the best part of being a volunteer driver.

*Barbara O'Mara*

## The Widow's Mite

I have been a driver for Northeast Austin Caregivers for a number of years and I have had many good experiences. More times than I can count, after I complete a drive or deliver a small Christmas package, the response would be, "God bless you for what you do."

My most memorable experience occurred when I drove an elderly woman for a doctor's visit in an office building that also had a pharmacy. After the doctor's visit, she asked me if we could stop by the pharmacy and check on a new prescription she had received. The pharmacist checked the prescription and told her there would be a co-pay. She checked her purse and then told him she would wait and get it later. When we arrived at her home, she handed me an envelope addressed to Northeast Austin Caregivers that contained money. My first reaction was to refuse the donation. I quickly realized that this act of giving was akin to the Biblical "Widow's Mite" and her pride would have been hurt if I did not accept it.

This woman knew that all our services are free but she was willing to delay getting her own medication to show her appreciation for what we do. That is an experience I will always remember.

*Boyd Covey*

*"The best part of being a volunteer driver is the joy it brings to my riders and the joy it brings to me to feel needed."*

Photograph courtesy of
*John Scurlock*

CHAPTER 10

# CROSSROADS
*I may need it someday*

> "*The best part of being a volunteer driver is being able to provide independence to some of the seniors who can no longer drive or have other limitations.*"

For many years, people have experimented with the development of programs in which people who volunteer today, build up credits which they can cash in tomorrow. The idea has been tried in several social service venues, including transportation. For the most part, they have faced huge barriers because of the need for record keeping, the perception that there would be no guarantee that their credits would be saved, the fear that a relocation might thwart the ability to "cash in" and, the general feeling that the point of volunteering is to give, not to receive.

**Do You Think You Will Be A Rider Someday?**

| | |
|---|---|
| Drivers | 77.8% |
| Organizations | 71.7% |
| Partners in Caregiving | 87.5% |

Vol. Drivers Who Believe They Will Be Riders Someday
*Beverly Foundation 2004 STAR Search Survey*

Volunteer driver stories throughout the book tell and retell the story that volunteer drivers feel that they receive more than they give. Their payment is in feeling needed and appreciated; experiencing satisfaction and inspiration; receiving hugs and kisses and kind words; sharing a meal and good conversation; and perhaps most important meeting new and interesting people.

While many volunteer drivers believe they may someday be riders, they appear to view their service not so much as "building up credits" as building a foundation for a program that will be there to serve them when they need it.

According to one driver:

> *"The best part of being a volunteer driver is seeing the hardships people have overcome. I am amazed. We older people are not fragile like so many are."*

## STORIES

### It Could Be Me

I moved to Fredericksburg, Texas in 1985 and within six months I became an active volunteer for the Hill Country Community Needs Council, a non-profit umbrella organization for lots of volunteer services, designed to serve people with a variety of needs. I had tried to develop such a program in the community where I had lived previously without positive results. I was excited about finding such an organization already functioning where I presently lived. I immediately began driving people to medical appointments within the city and to surrounding cities as far as ninety miles away.

Almost every time I took a client, the client would say - sometimes in tears -"I don't know what I would do without the Needs Council's help. When I learned that I needed treatments, I had no family in town and no way to drive myself to the doctor. Without you, I would have been unable to get the treatment I needed." The trip seemed so easy for me, even when it took hours of my time, but to the client it was huge. I have helped clients receive radiation treatments, dialysis treatments, eye surgeries, check ups after surgery, and other treatments requiring trips out of town. One of the clients that I have driven to a doctor multiple times is a Hispanic woman who speaks no English.

Always when we get back to her house she smiles and gives me a big hug—her way of saying "thank you". Another client is blind, has only one leg and requires additional treatments at a Veterans' hospital in a neighboring town. Although he has many limitations, he never fails to be positive and pleasant about his situation. These people encourage me and help me to realize how very blessed I am. I just hope that there will be an organization available for me, if the need arises, that will serve my needs in such a caring way, maintaining my dignity no matter what problems I face.

*Peggy Benson*

## What Goes Around Comes Around

It's hard to put into one to two paragraphs how this driving has changed my life, but here goes. Riders, as you call them, think of us as angels, but they don't realize how they change our lives. I've become a better listener as some of these riders have no one to talk to, and by the time your trip is over you know their history. Where they were born, all about their family, they love to visit with you, and sometimes they even confide in you, or ask your opinion about a problem. I also don't find myself complaining as much, as most of them are so much worse off than I. Most of the riders are very sick, but they want to be treated with respect and dignity, and that is what we do.

Most of our people end up adopting us, if they like you they want you and only you to take them. Also we always receive birthday cards, Christmas cards, etc. They make you feel so important in their lives. These are the benefits of volunteer driving, or doing any kind of volunteer work. You are tired when you go to bed at night, but you feel good about yourself, and that you have probably made someone happy today, by listening to them, and treating them with kindness. I believe that what goes around comes around, and I know some day I will need this service, and there will be someone there for me.

*Donna Moberley*

## Some People Team It

The best part of being a volunteer driver is having the time and being able to help people who have no way of getting to their doctor appointments, and receiving their appreciation. My wife always goes with me, and one lady we took to and returned from dialysis at the University of Iowa over 100 times. She always thanked us regardless of how she felt, whether it was a good day or a bad day. She is now deceased.

Sometime in the future, we may need the same service because we live in a small town 30 to 45 miles from hospitals and major specialist doctors.

*Wilbert "Webb" Thoeming*

## Personal Satisfaction

I enjoy being a volunteer... being able to help seniors who are not able to drive anymore and who want to get out of the house to visit with people or to be taken for medical appointments. It gives me much personal satisfaction knowing that one day I also may be in the same situation and hoping there may be someone who will treat me with the same respect and dignity that I have shown the people I volunteer with. I have only been in Arizona for a few years after spending my entire life in Northern Minnesota. The program has given me an opportunity to meet many fine people.

*Gillette K. Amidon*

## Chauffeuring Special People

Adjusting to not driving is a major challenge in a senior's life. It's hard to have to rely on others to get from place to place. Loss of one's independence is a big loss. A lot of seniors feel like they are a burden on others by having to ask for a ride especially after all those years of being independent. Coming and going as one pleases is taken for granted by most of us.

I try to be cheerful and up beat with my riders. I remind them that I don't have to drive – I want to. I tell them after all these years they finally have a chauffer and a vehicle at their disposal just like the rich people. I try to make them feel special. I open doors for them. I sometimes help them shop or read labels. I want their trip to be fun, like going some place with a buddy. We tell jokes, share memories and basically try to get comfortable with each other. Sometimes we take the longgggg way home, just so they can look at "stuff." I look forward to caring for my riders. I hope their day is just a little bit better by riding with me. I know that some day I may need a ride.

*Kenneth Dickinson*

*"The best part of being a volunteer driver is the feeling of self-worth and discovering most people care about the same things in life."*

Photograph courtesy of
*Lila Jue*

# APPENDICES
*Table of Contents*

Appendix I
# Biographies of Winners
*Stories of Excellence*

*Patricia Britt*

Patricia Britt is very involved with many activities in the San Diego area; she is head of a twenty-two team marathon bridge group called "Bridge-O-Rama;" she is a Senior Driver, and is active in multiple Bridge/Scrabble/Poker/Bingo groups.

Pat is proud of being a member of the Traditional Choir at St. Elizabeth Seton Church in Carlsbad, California. They participated in a singing pilgrimage to Fatima, Portugal, Madrid, and Paris this last summer.

But first in line for her time and love are her four children, and eight grandchildren.

*Virginia Burns*

Virginia Law Burns has worn many hats during her lifetime. Some of them include: driving an Army truck during World

War II, a factory worker, waitress, and elementary school teacher. At this time, her three children are grown and have given her a dozen quite wonderful grandkids.

Virginia lives in a rural area of Mid-Michigan on a high meadow that slopes to a woods and a friendly river. In addition to her volunteer activities her hobbies are communing with wildlife, flower gardening, cat-sitting, writing poetry, and singing with a country band.

 *Gena Morrow*

Gena identifies herself as a Mother, a Grandmother, a sister, an aunt, a niece, a cousin, and a friend to my favorite people. She is proud to be a retired rural carrier for the U.S. Post office and a volunteer driver for those who need a ride as well as a volunteer at the hospital for those who need assistance. She enjoys life!

## Appendix II
# Index of Authors
*Listed alphabetically by last name*

41　***Patricia Britt (winner)***
Encinitas Out and About Senior Transportation Program:
Encinitas, CA

　3　***Virginia Burns (winner)***
Looking Glass Community Services – Volunteer Taxi:
Laingsburg, MI

79　***Dariek Calloway***
CART Volunteer Driver Program: Harrisonburg, VA

66　***Sarah Carriker***
West Austin Caregivers: Austin, TX

35　***Richard Chesbrough***
Neighborhood Senior Services Medical Access Program:
Ann Arbor, MI

67　***John Conrado***
South Austin Caregivers, Inc.: Austin, TX

90　***Boyd Covey***
Caregivers of Northeast Austin: Austin, TX

98　***Kenneth Dickinson***
Clio Area Senior Center Van Transportation Program:
Clio, MI

67　***Olivia Donelson***
West Austin Caregivers: Austin, TX

35　***David Draggoo***
Looking Glass Community Services – Volunteer Taxi:
Laingsburg, MI

87　***Gordon Easlick***
Looking Glass Community Services – Volunteer Taxi:
Laingsburg, MI

76　***Catharine F. Edgerton***
Peninsula Shepherd Senior Center: San Diego, CA

24　***Susan Elke***
Effingham County FISH Human Services: Effingham, IL

48  **Beth Holl**
Barton County Interfaith Volunteers in Action:
Great Bend, KS

4  **Edward Honcik**
Freemont Car-Go/ Blair Car-Go: Freemont, NE

13  **William Hubbard**
COAST: Colfax, WA

34  **Brian C. Irslinger**
Retired and Senior Volunteer Program of Schuylkill
County: Pottsville, PA

77  **Brian C. Irslinger**
Retired and Senior Volunteer Program of Schuylkill
County: Pottsville, PA

49  **Anita Jensen**
Lend A Hand: Boulder City, NV

28  **Don Johnson**
Rural Transportation Program at Joint Council for Economic Opportunity, funded by Clinton County Office for
the Aging: Plattsburgh, NY

74  **Margaret Johnston**
Volunteer Services of Cedar County: Tipton, IA

56  **Kathy Jones**
Benton County Senior Citizens Dial-A-Bus: Corvallis, OR

88  **Lila Jue**
Evergreen Senior Center: Northridge, CA

47  **Eldon Kaufman**
Macomb County Interfaith Volunteer Caregivers:
Macomb, MI

71  **Tom King**
Volunteer Center of Jefferson County, Inc.:
Watertown, NY

47  **Billy Moberley**
Gold County Telecare, Inc.; Neighbor-To-Neighbor Volunteer Driver Program: Grass Valley, CA

96  **Donna Moberley**
Gold County Telecare, Inc.; Neighbor-To-Neighbor Volunteer Driver Program: Grass Valley, CA

55  **Gena Morrow (winner)**
Call A Ride, Inc.: Hebron, IN

59  **Zenada Morrow**
Call A Ride, Inc.: Hebron, IN

7  **Dean Murphy**
H & C Burnside Senior Center Van Service: Coldwater, MI

63  **Betty Newell**
CART Volunteer Driver Program: Harrisonburg, VA

89  **Barbara O'Mara**
Macomb County Interfaith Volunteer Caregivers: Macomb, MI

56  **Ernest V. Oakley**
Rural Transportation Program at Joint Council for Economic Opportunity, funded by Clinton County Office for the Aging: Plattsburgh, NY

78  **Ernest V. Oakley**
Rural Transportation Program at Joint Council For Economic Opportunity, funded by Clinton County Office for the Aging: Plattsburgh, NY

50  **Evelyn Palmer**
Grafton County Senior Citizens Council, Inc.: Lebanon, NH

58  **Mary Ann Palmer**
Round Rock Caregivers: Round Rock, TX

49  **Wilma Pearson**
Volunteer Services of Cedar County: Tipton, IA

73 **Sharion Tanner**
Faith in Action Pflugerville Caregivers: Pflugerville, TX

17 **Jennifer Teel**
West Austin Caregivers: Austin, TX

97 **Wilbert "Webb" Thoeming**
Volunteer Services of Cedar County: Tipton, IA

13 **Gary Tiedeman**
Benton County Senior Citizens Dial-A-Bus: Corvallis, OR

15 **Joan Tomlinson**
Project LIVE (Living Independently through Volunteer Efforts): Knoxville, TN

7 **Tom & Phyllis Tomlinson**
Round Rock Caregivers: Round Rock, TX

45 **John Veskerna**
Peninsula Shepherd Senior Center: San Diego, CA

31 **Alfred Wilke**
Granby Senior Van Program: Granby, CT

45 **John Williams, Jr.**
TRIP (Transportation Reimbursement & Information Project): Riverside, CA

27 **Charles Wright**
Peninsula Shepherd Senior Center: San Diego, CA

16 **Allison Wylot**
Encinitas Out and About Senior Transportation Program: Encinitas, CA

Appendix III

# Index of Stories

*Listed by chapter*

**3: Two Way Street**

## 5: The Extra Mile

## 7: The Long Way Home

## 8: Passages

## 9: The High Road

Appendix IV

# Index of Organizations
*Volunteer Driver Programs*

**Barton County Interfaith Volunteers in Action**
Great Bend, KS

**Benton County Senior Citizens Dial-A-Bus**
Corvallis, OR

**Call A Ride, Inc.**
Hebron, IN

**Caregivers of Northeast Austin**
Austin, TX

**CART Volunteer Driver Program**
Harrisonburg, VA

**Chore Connection, Mid County Senior Services**
Newtown Square, PA

**Clio Area Senior Center Van Transportation Program**
Clio, MI

**COAST**
Colfax, WA

**Effingham County FISH Human Services**
Effingham, IL

**Encinitas Out and About Senior Transportation Program**
Encinitas, CA

**Evergreen Senior Center**
Northridge, CA

**Faith in Action Pflugerville Caregivers**
Pflugerville, TX

**Freemont Car-Go/ Blair Car-Go**
Freemont, NE

**Gold County Telecare, Inc.**
**Neighbor-To-Neighbor Volunteer Driver Program**
Grass Valley, CA

**Grafton County Senior Citizens Council, Inc.**
Lebanon, NH

**Granby Senior Van Program**
Granby, CT

**H & C Burnside Senior Center Van Service**
Coldwater, MI

**Hill Country Community Needs Council**
Hill Country, TX

**Johnson County Catch-A-Ride**
Olathe, KS

**KeoweeCares**
Salem, SC

**Kindness, Inc.**
Mountain Home, AR

**Lend A Hand**
Boulder City, NV

**Lighthouse Emergency Services: Senior Services**
Pontiac, MI

**Looking Glass Community Services—Volunteer Taxi**
Laingsburg, MI

**Macomb County Interfaith Volunteer Caregivers**
Macomb, MI

**Neighborhood Senior Services Medical Access Program**
Ann Arbor, MI

**North Central Caregivers**
Austin, TX

**Peninsula Shepherd Senior Center**
San Diego, CA

**Project HEARTH (Helping Elderly Adults Remain in Their Homes)**
Pottstown, PA

**Project LIVE (Living Independently through Volunteer Efforts)**
Knoxville, TN

**Retired and Senior Volunteer Program of Schuylkill County**
Pottsville, PA

**Round Rock Caregivers**
Round Rock, TX

**RSVP of Central Oklahoma, Inc.**
Oklahoma City, OK

**Rural Transportation Program at Joint Council for Economic Opportunity, funded by Clinton County Office for the Aging**
Plattsburgh, NY

**Shepherd's Center of Raytown**
Kansas City, MO

**South Austin Caregivers, Inc.**
Austin, TX

**Surprise Senior Center**
Surprise, AZ

**The Deposit Foundation Transportation Program**
Deposit, NY

**The Volunteer Center of Lewis, Mason and Thurston Counties**
Thurston, WA

**Tri-Cities Faith in Action**
Granite City, IL

**TRIP (Transportation Reimbursement & Information Project)**
Riverside, CA

**Volunteer Center of Jefferson County, Inc.**
Watertown, NY

**Volunteer Services of Cedar County**
Tipton, IA

**West Austin Caregivers**
Austin, TX

**Appendix V**

# 20 Ways

*To become a volunteer driver*

People often say, "I enjoy knowing what other people do and why they do it, but what I would really like to know is, how do I get started?" Here's how several people say they got involved in volunteer driver programs.

1. "My RSVP stationed me at a volunteer driver program."

2. "I was a Meals-on-Wheels driver and then decided to drive people rather than food."

3. "I was helping my neighbor, and a volunteer driver program found out about me and asked me to drive every so often."

4. "My neighbor asked me to take her to the store, and we made it a weekly routine."

5. "My minister asked me to help one of our church members."

6. "I agreed to volunteer with a program, and all of a sudden I was a volunteer driver."

7. "My auxiliary started a program and I participated to get service credits."

8. "I heard about it at my driver training workshop."

9. "I found out about it from a neighbor, completely by accident."

10. "I was working at the senior center and someone talked about the volunteer driver program and got me started."

11. "I called my local area agency on aging and they referred me to a program."

12. "I put my name on the board at the senior center and they contacted me."

13. "I responded to an advertisement in the paper."

14. "I started a volunteer driver program."

15. "I looked on the web for a program in my community."

16. "I contacted my local Automobile Association (unit) and received information about a local program."

17. "I drove someone in my church, and eventually started driving several people."

18. "First I was a paid driver and I realized the need... so when I was asked by a friend, I said yes."

19. "There was nothing else for me to do after retirement... I sat around for two years and then Marge asked me to drive."

20. "I lost my husband and son, and was depressed, so a friend said lets give something back to people who helped us... and got me out to do volunteer activities."

It is clear from these comments that while it is possible to aggressively seek out volunteer driver programs, many people are sought out by them, or simply start by volunteering to drive a friend.

The Trustees and staff of the Beverly Foundation believe that mobility and transportation are two of the critical challenges facing older Americans.

Seniors who are mobile can sit and stand and move about. When they have transportation, seniors can get where they need to go. However, seniors say that conditions that limit their transportation limit their lives. At the Beverly Foundation, new ideas and options are fostered to enhance mobility and transportation for today's and tomorrows' older population.

To learn more about the Beverly Foundation, and its senior transportation and annual STAR Search and STAR Awards programs, visit us online at:

www.beverlyfoundation.org